Technology Enhanced Teaching

Framework for onsite teaching
with multiple devices

1st Edition

First edition published 2016
by Mazohl Publishing
H.O. Staglgasse 13, A-2700 Wiener Neustadt, Austria

© 2016 Peter Mazohl

The right of the editors to be identified as the author of the editorial material, and of the authors for their individual chapters, has been asserted in accordance with sections 77 and 78 of the Copyright, Designs and Patents Act 1988 of the USA.

All rights reserved. No part of this book may be reprinted or reproduced or utilized in any form or by any electronic, mechanical, or other means, now known or hereafter invented, including photocopying and recording, or in any information storage or retrieval system, without permission in writing from the publishers.

Trademark notice: Product or corporate names may be trademarks or registered trademarks, and are used only for identification and explanation without intent to infringe.

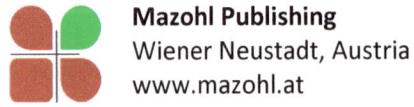

Mazohl Publishing
Wiener Neustadt, Austria
www.mazohl.at

ISBN: 978-3-901679-21-6
Typeset in Calibri by Peter Mazohl
Graphics by Peter Mazohl
Cover image © Peter Mazohl 2016

Contents

1 **TEACHING AND LEARNING PRECONDITIONS** 1

    1.1   Traditional Teaching at Traditional Austrian High Schools 1
    1.2   Description of the School 2
    1.3   Description of the Students 4
    1.4   Description of the Curriculum 4
    1.5   Background of the Study – Statistical Information 5

2 **PEDAGOGICAL APPROACH AND INSTRUCTIONAL DESIGN** 7

    2.1   Considerations about Didactic 7
    2.2   Instructional Design 9
    2.3   Learner-centered Access 18
    2.4   Competence based learning outcomes 20
    2.5   Use of Multimedia 23
    2.6   Assessments and Grading 25
    2.7   Evaluation of Courses 28

3 **LEARNING AND TEACHING ENVIRONMENT** 31

    3.1   Necessary Infrastructure 31
    3.2   Students' Equipment 33
    3.3   Students Pre-Knowledge 34
    3.4   Learning Platform 37
    3.5   Classroom and Labs 41

4 **TEACHING EXPERIENCE** 45

    4.1   The Teaching Method 45
    4.2   Preparation Work 47
    4.3   Sample Chapter Creation 53
    4.4   Students' Needs 55
    4.5   Students' Involvement 58
    4.6   Motivation 63
    4.7   Assessment 65
    4.8   Results 69

5 STUDENTS' FEEDBACK 72
- 5.1 Empirical Research 72
- 5.2 Open Questions 102
- 5.3 Summary 105

6 LESSONS LEARNED 107
- 6.1 Pros – Cons Balance 107
- 6.2 Multimedia and Interactive Materials 109
- 6.3 Group Work and Discussions 111
- 6.4 Distance Learning 114
- 6.5 Pedagogical considerations 115
- 6.6 Problems with the Infrastructure 121
- 6.7 What Students Need 123

7 TRANSFERABILITY GUIDE 127
- 7.1 Pedagogical Approach 127
- 7.2 Versatile use in Different Fields of Education 128
- 7.3 Subject Related Issues 131
- 7.4 Related Software 134
- 7.5 eLearning Platform 135
- 7.6 Assessment 136
- 7.7 Blended Learning 136

8 REFERENCES 137

Preface

This book describes a technology enhanced teaching method developed during the last 8 years in an Austrian high school with students' age between 16 and 18 years old.

The system was developed out of a Grundtvig Learning Partnership and enhanced and amended during the last years. The developed and practiced teaching method can easily be transferred to any other country in which technology enhanced teaching (or training) is relevant.

In the same way the method is not fixed to school education in high schools but can be used as well in Higher Education and can be a splendid method in Adult Education.

The book is split into seven chapters:

Learning and teaching preconditions

>This chapter gives attention to the teaching preconditions in a typical Austrian high school covering the onsite teaching settings as well as the students and the curriculum of the taught subject called "Physics".

Pedagogical access and instructional design

>Here the ideas and background knowledge of the teaching approach are briefly summarized and described.

Learning and teaching environment

>This section describes the necessary infrastructure, the equipment, students' pre-knowledge, the used learning platform, and finally the classrooms and labs.

Teaching experience

>In this chapter, the method is described in detail including samples and a self-evaluation of the teaching.

Students' feedback
> This part in the book gives an overview of the evaluation of the teaching method. Here the results of two questionnaires provide a realistic feedback of the students.

Lessons learned
> Here you find a conclusion of the teaching experience. Here also a pros/cons analyses are provided. Several items of chapter 2 are also critically discussed and proposals for further development are given.

Transferability guide
> This chapter covers considerations, ideas and hints to transfer the described method to either other subject or to other fields of education.

1 Teaching and Learning Preconditions

Since more than 45 years I am working in the field of education teaching science. I started with lessons in mathematics and physics and in the 1980s I started teaching Informatics. Graphics, multimedia and the production of media started to play an important role in my life. Some years later I realized the enormous potential, which is hidden in ICT and the technology behind, and I started to develop training programs using a computer as a training tool and learning aid.

This book describes and discusses the teaching method developed in the last ten years and the implementation of this method in teaching physics in an upper high school.

1.1 Traditional Teaching at Traditional Austrian High Schools

Traditional teaching means ex-cathedra lessons of physics or special lab-based class. This method is highly efficient and was used by teachers for the last decades.

New pedagogical streams were taken in account, like project based teaching or a student-centered learning with special hands-on experiments performed by the students.

Nothing changed the teaching more as the appearance of technology in class. The availability of computers changed existing teaching practices. The first scientific publications dealing with technology as an element in teaching and learning can be found between 2007 and 2009. Kirkwood & Price (2013) give an excellent overview describing the attempts of implementing Technology Enhanced Learning (TEL).

1.2 Description of the School

The school, in which I have been teaching for the last years, is a typical grammar school (in Austria called "Gymnasium"). The pupils enter school at an age of ten and leave the school as students with 18. The final exams (or school-leaving examination) give them the right to start to study at any university or university of applied sciences or any other education of tertiary education.

The school time is split into two periods, the lower level (10 – 14 years old pupils) and the upper level (15 – 18 years old students). Over all, approximately 650 people attend these two levels, approximately 400 in the lower and 250 in the upper level. In the upper level, approximately 90% are female students (reason unknown).

All students attend Latin lessons for 6 years. English is the currently taught modern language for 8 years.

1.2.1 Structure of the learning

The eight years of learning are split in a lower and an upper level (similar to a secondary high school). At the upper level in average 20 – 25 students attend the classes. All lessons are run as technology enhanced classes. This means that the students use their own laptop or other multiple devices as means of learning in all subjects.

1.2.2 eLearning

The school is an eLearning Cluster School. This means that eLearning should be practiced intensively and an intensive knowledge exchange should be performed between the schools belonging to the cluster. However, this idealistic goal failed due to the insufficient education of teachers and missing concepts of the Ministry of Education as well as the missing coordination and leadership of the heads in charge at the school.

For students and teachers exist an eLearning platform based on Moodle, but this system is used poorly due to the obstacles mentioned before.

1.2.3 Daily teaching flow

Each lesson lasts 50 minutes, an average school week for students covers ± 30 lessons in a five-day week, and the teaching during a school year covers ± 38 weeks. The lessons normally end at 13:10 o'clock, the compulsory optional subjects (which can be selected by students up from the 6th form) are taught in the afternoon.

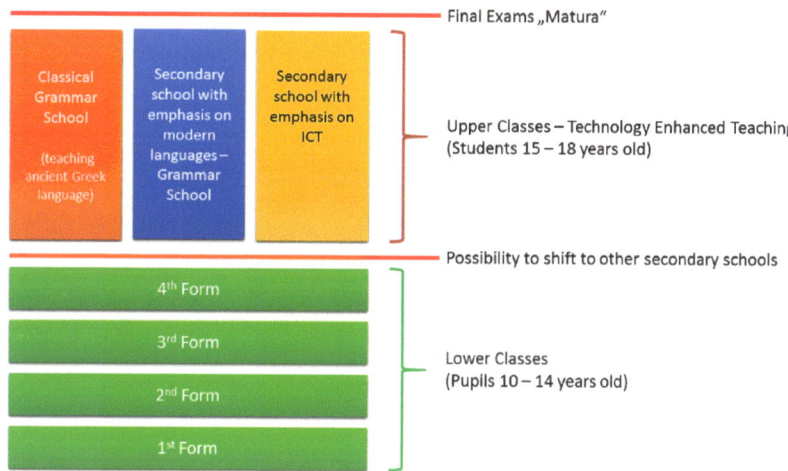

Figure 1: *The School Structure*

Hint: Due to the situation that people in Austria have finished the compulsory school education with an age of 15 (after having passed nine school years), the term "pupil" is used for children in compulsory education. The term "student" is used for teenagers being involved in secondary education (attending the school on their free will additional to the compulsory engagement). The average age to finish secondary education with final exams that enables to study at a university is 18 years (up to 19 years) old.[1]

---

[1] Further information about the Austrian Education System is available from http://www.bildungssystem.at/en/ in English language. The page offers an interactive access to a very detailed description of the educational system.

1.3 Description of the Students

The students involved in the training are 15 to 18 years old. They all have a special ICT education which is - more or less - equivalent to the ECDL (at basic level)[2] and many students passed the ECDL exams. Furthermore, they get a special education in Presentation Technics and Project Management (teaching one year with either 35 lessons the year or 70 lessons, depending of the selected emphasis).

They also learned type writing (with ten fingers[3]) and should be able to make notes on the computer with a word processing software by writing of a speed of 100 characters per minute.

All students learn English as the first foreign language and leave the school with a minimum level of B2[4], many of the students reach the level C1. That means that they can follow native speakers in videos or presentations without help from the teacher. Sometimes they need some instructions or explication of special terms or words because the technical vocabulary is not taught so intensively in the language lessons.

1.4 Description of the Curriculum

This book refers to the teaching of physics in a typical Austrian "Gymnasium" as described above.

---

[2] European Computer Driving License
[3] 10-finger touch typing means that students can write with a speed up to 100 characters per minute without looking at the keyboard.
[4] See: http://www.coe.int/t/dg4/linguistic/Cadre1_en.asp
B2 is defined as: Can understand the main ideas of complex text on both concrete and abstract topics, including technical discussions in his/her field of specialization. Can interact with a degree of fluency and spontaneity that makes regular interaction with native speakers quite possible without strain for either party. Can produce clear, detailed text on a wide range of subjects and explain a viewpoint on a topical issue giving the advantages and disadvantages of various options.

The curriculum is competence based and describes the didactic principles, the learning goals and the learning objectives [5]. A central statement describes the educational principles:

> *Das Ziel ist der Erwerb folgender Fähigkeiten,*
> *Fertigkeiten und Werthaltungen*[6]

This is basically the definition of a competence. The difference to the common used definition is the use of abilities instead of knowledge.

The reason can be found in the fact that the curriculum in Austria was content driven for many years. That means, that knowledge was the centre of all learning activities. Obviously, the responsible people were afraid to use the term knowledge again and replaced that by abilities.

From the point of view of a teacher working for more than 40 years in various educational systems skills are impossible without knowledge.

Another interesting issue is the description of related topics in the curriculum. Physics should be seen as science with an impact to nature and technics, language and communication, and society. Other addressed issues are creativity and figuration as well as health and exercise.

In the general statement listed above more items than the simple teaching of a subject is included. It addresses the building of digital competence as well as critical thinking and problem solving or social competence (to be able to learn in groups).

1.5   Background of the Study – Statistical Information

The sample covers approximately 76 students with an age variant from 16 to 18 years old. The majority are female students depending of the chosen type of school. In the linguistic type, up to 95 % are female; in the ICT type, approximately 50 % of the students are female.

From 76 students 72 answered the survey. The used program was LimeSurvey[7], an open source tool with a sophisticated user management

---

[5] https://www.bmbf.gv.at/schulen/unterricht/lp/lp_neu_ahs_10_11862.pdf?4dzgm2, page 1

[6] **Translation**: The aim is the acquirement of the abilities, skills and attitudes

[7] https://www.limesurvey.org/

supporting both anonymous and not-anonymous surveys. The tool supports up to 28 different question types, offers an efficient export to analyse tools like R[8].

The data processing was done with R and Excel.

Additional data was collected in focus groups. These were performed either to confirm the findings from the survey as well as to get additional information from a broad scope of concerned students. Approximately 100 students have been taking part at the focus groups, split in six groups with ten to twenty students per group.

LimeSurvey is the most used open source tool for professional surveys.

[8] https://www.r-project.org/
R is a free software environment for statistical computing and graphics.

2 Pedagogical Approach and Instructional Design

Pedagogy often is seen as the art and science of teaching. The origin of the term comes from the Greek language and means children education. Today we live in a time of permanent learning. Lifelong Learning is a fact and well established in society. Besides that, it is a fixed item in the European landscape of education, and not only here. From the current and modern view pedagogy is used to guide (or to lead) learners (of all ages). That causes a shifting of the function and the role of teachers from a source of knowledge to a facilitator of the learning process.

This chapter gives a summary of ideas, methods and considerations for the pedagogical approach to the described method in technology enhanced training. The methodology of the pedagogical approach is to analyze existing pedagogical streams, theories or ideas, to select the best fitting items or parts out of them and to combine them to an appropriate and well-fitting pedagogical framework.

2.1 Considerations about Didactic

During the past century, various didactical methods were developed based on psychological research and developed learning theories. Well known are the behaviorist method as well as the constructivist teaching.
Behaviorism focus on learning and conditioning.
The constructivist access provides an active involvement of learners with interactive and student-centered activities. The teacher acts as a facilitator of the students' learning process and encourages the learners to act responsible and autonomous.

2.1.1 What does teaching mean?

Richard Felder (2002) mentions in an interview two different meanings of teaching:

> *First, it can simply mean presenting information, so*
> *that if I lecture on something I can say that I taught it,*
> *whether or not anyone learned it. The second meaning*
> *of teaching is "helping someone to learn."*
> *According to this meaning - which I personally accept -*
> *if I lecture on something and the students don't learn it,*
> *I have not taught it.*

Pia Petersen (2004) means that a teacher needs knowledge of both teaching and learning. In the last years, the focus shifted from teaching to learning. Teachers take in account the situation of learners and try to support the learners best.

2.1.2 Importance and influence of didactics

The Czech scholar Johan Amos Comenius (1592-1670) is one of the most famous founder of General Didactics in Europe. He published his "Didacta Magna" ("Great Didactics") in 1657 and up to now the content builds a guideline and inspiration for didactical thinking.

The educational landscape has been changed and technology integrated in teaching and learning forced a different didactical approach. Hilbert Meyer (2014) explained this and the current status of didactic (in Germany and in context of European countries) in his speech "The German Tradition of Didactics and Recent Research Findings about Teaching and Learning" at the 12th International Curriculum Forum (in Shanghai). He promotes the importance of self-reflection (both of learners and teachers) as an emphasis of modern didactics.

This emphasis can be found as a typical issue in today's learner-centered learning.

2.1.3 Didactic competences of teachers

A teacher must have certain didactic competences to act successfully. Some people are natural talents; others have to learn these didactic competences during their studies.

In modern teaching, some issues seem to be important:
- The ability to create a suitable curriculum based on the competences learners have to gain or to transfer a given curriculum suitable to the learning
- Teachers must have the competence to act in different roles, for example explaining, motivating, coaching, responding, as a role model, and others.
- Teachers must have the competence to evaluate and to reflect (that includes also the items of self-evaluation and self-reflection).

Evaluation and reflection of the own teaching in context with the learning results are an important issue in a quality enhancement system.

2.2 Instructional Design

Educators spend a lot of their time creating effective lessons. Today it is essential to meet the needs of all students or learners, to engage them actively and to provide them with modern multimedia based and interactive learning material. This all needs a serious and intensive planning using different types of instructional models.

Instructional design has its origin in the training of military members and was based on instruction, learning, and human behavior. From that access it is in opposition to the current way of teaching in which competences are in the foreground and not a military drill but the understanding of context and personal skills grows more and more important. Nevertheless, also in competence oriented teaching and learning a certain effort invested in the planning and structure of lessons is necessary. Therefore, instructional design still has its place in the development of lessons and courses.

The four models mentioned here provide a promising access to design courses or lessons and were used for the development of the teaching method (taking out the best of all).

2.2.1 The ADDIE Model

A very popular model is the ADDIE process which was developed at the Florida State University in the late 1980. ADDIE stands for

- **Analyses** = Identification of the instructional problem, analyzes of learner characteristics, competences to be learned and other items.
- **Design** = defines learning objectives and the content (competences), the assessments, exercises, planning of lessons or the use of different media.
- **Development** = creating of the instructional or training materials as designed
- **Implementation** = training of facilitators/trainers and the learners and other preparation work like availability of materials, books and other instructional resources.
- **Evaluation** = formative evaluation (after each stage of the ADDIE) and summative evaluation of the training (including a feedback from the learners) make sure the materials meet the desired goals.

The model works linear, but it is drawn as a circle in the figure to demonstrate the option of a continuous quality enhancement by using the evaluation results for amendments in the next cycle. Branch (2008) gives a comprehensive overview to the ADDIE model.

Figure 2: Addie Model

The ADDIE Model offers still an appropriate way to implement training. It also can be used for competence oriented training. It describes the various elements as individual items which are executed one after the other. It is possible to integrate amendment processes using ADDIE as a kind of amendment cycle.

The described teaching model follows the ADDIE model implementing several enhancements taken from the other models described in this chapter.

2.2.2 The Dick and Carey Model (1996)

This model bases on the interconnection of each part of an instructional design process to others. So the design process shows the relations between the acting people and the organizational items. The access to instructional design is systematic and includes feedback cycles which can be used for amendments. The idea uses ten parts which are connected in a certain relation and dependency. Dick and Carey mentioned that the instructor, learners, materials, instructional activities, the delivery system, learning, and the performance environments interact with each other to reach the desired learners' outcomes (Dick, 2015)

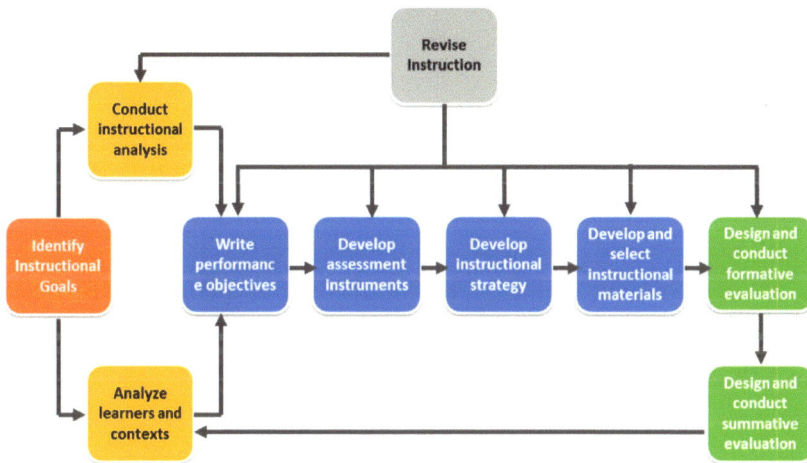

Figure 3: *Dick Carey Model*

1. Assess needs to **identify instructional goal**(s)
   Determine what learners are expected to be able to perform at the end of instruction.
   Hint: This access enables a competence oriented model of learning.
2. **Conduct instructional analysis**
   to determine a step-by-step of what learners are doing when they

are performing the goal;
to determine what skills and knowledge are required

3. **Analyze learners and contexts / identify entry behaviors**
   Identify learners' present skills, preferences and attitude as well as the characteristics of the instructional setting. Identify with which skills and attitudes the learners will enter the learning task. This are typical ingredients of competence oriented learning.
   The collected facts include the useful information about the target learners and include entry behaviors, prior knowledge of the topic area, attitudes toward content and potential delivery systems (for example learning platforms), general motivation and other relevant items

4. **Write performance objectives**
   Transform the needs and goals of the tasks into clear objectives to specify what the learners will be able to do with the learned skills

5. **Develop assessment instruments** or **criterion-oriented tests**
   Development of criteria-referenced assessments consistent with the performance objectives defined above. They are used to assess the progress during the learning process.

6. **Develop instructional strategy**
   Development of strategies and activities to achieve the objectives
   This includes items like motivation, objectives and entry behavior, the presentation of information (for example instructional sequence, information, examples), learner's participation (practice and feedback), testing (often done with a pretest and posttest to evaluate the knowledge or competence enhancement of learners) and follow-through activities (remediation, enrichment, memorization and transfer)

7. **Develop and select instructional materials**
   Determine what instructional materials will be used.

8. **Design and conduct formative evaluation**
   Data is collected to identify how the designed instructional material can be improved and to expand the effectiveness of the instruction to a bigger audience.

9. **Revise Instruction**
   Here the data from the formative evaluation is used to examine the validity of the instructional analysis, learner and context analysis, performance objectives, assessment instruments, instructional strategies, and instruction.
   This is part of an included quality enhancement cycle.
10. **Design and conduct summative evaluation**
   This part is used to analyze the quality of the system as a whole and to measure the value and success of the instruction.

The elements of the ADDIE Model can be found in the Dick & Carey Model as well, but is more detailed in any sense. This model could be used in a classroom or distance learning or in the business world, for example in VET continuous education.

The system carries a versatile concept and can be used in schools for teaching as well as in the business world for employees' training and also in Adult Education.

On the other hand, the system forces to invest a lot of time. Furthermore, it does not support variable parameters like various outcomes of the learners' analyses. Therefore, the design must be completely redesigned in dependency of different analyses results.

2.2.3 Kemp's Instructional Design Model M-R-K (1977)

The Morrison, Ross, and Kemp Model (2004) is commonly known as the Kemp Model. It is an instructional design model with focus on the adoption of continuous implementation. Evaluation is done through the instructional design process. Kemp promotes an access to instructional design as a continuous cycle with revision as an ongoing activity in close context with all the other elements.

The Kemp Design Model consists of 9 steps:

1. **Identify instructional problems**, and specify goals for designing an instructional program.
2. **Examine learner characteristics** that should receive attention during planning.

3. **Identify subject content**, and analyze task components related to stated goals and purposes.
4. **State instructional objectives** for the learner.
5. **Sequence content** within each instructional unit for logical learning.
6. **Design instructional strategies** so that each learner can master the objectives.
7. **Plan** the **instructional message** and **delivery**.
8. **Develop evaluation instruments** to assess objectives.
9. **Select resources** to support instruction and learning activities.

The Kemp Model includes all elements of the ADDIE Model and therefore looks like a little bit like an extension of the ADDIE Model. The difference is that the ADDIE Model is more linear with a step-by-step process while the Kemp Model provides a non-linear development allowing constantly done revisions all the time at each area.

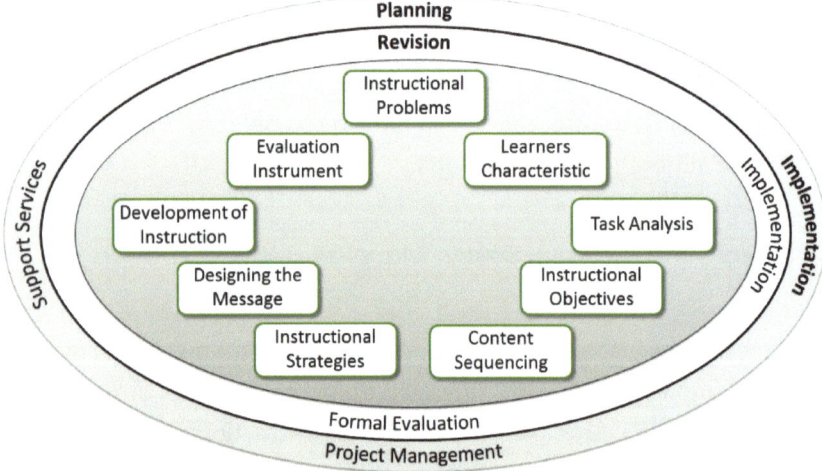

Figure 4: The Kemp Model

This model can also be used for curriculum as well as for individual lessons. From this model item 6 (Design instructional strategies so that each learner can master the objectives) and item 7 (Plan the instructional message and delivery) were integrated in the teaching method.

Especially item 6 was the source to develop the packages of material for the learner (see chapter 4.1)

2.2.4 Cathy Moore's Action Mapping (2008)

The Action Mapping model (2013) includes four items or steps which create the base of your action map for course creation:

1. **Identify the learning** (or business) **goal**
   Focusing on the goal means to explain what learners finally have to do (or to know) instead of supplying the learners with simple information. Unnecessary information is avoided and the learners may concentrate on the most essential points of their future job.

2. **Identify what people need to do**
   Here you find out which steps or actions are necessary for the involved people to achieve the learning (or business) aim. These steps indicate necessary actions instead of simple information or pure knowledge.

3. **Design practice activities**
   Practice activities are related to real tasks or activities, which people are going to perform at their working place or as a result of their learning.

4. **Identify what people really need to know**
   This is a kind of optimizing process in which you collect the minimum amount of information which the learners have to keep in mind in order to complete each practice activity (this information must also be available in the further job or implementation of the learning outcomes.

Action Mapping is often seen as a modern method to create eLearning courses or trainings in companies. The core idea is not to define what people have to know but to explain what people have to do (to reach a defined goal). In most descriptions a business goal is mentioned but any learning goal can be used instead.

Action Maps are non-linear descriptions of a course. They are similar to mind maps and mind mapping tools can be used to create an action map.

From this model the item 4 was used as an analyses tool to define the content of the material package students get to be supported in taking notes (see chapter 4.1).

2.2.5 Other models

Here are several other models which have been taken into consideration for the development of the pedagogical framework and have given some impact in the implementation phase of the framework.

- **Gagné's 9 Events of Instruction**
  In this instructional design model a behavioristic as well as a cognitivist approach can be realized. The model uses basic "conditions of learning" and breaks these down into internal and external conditions. Internal conditions deal with the learned capabilities of the learner, external conditions work as "stimuli" for the learner.
  The method can be used for complete courses as well as for single lessons or eLearning activities.
  More information can be found in "Principles of Instructional Design" by Robert Gagné (2004)

- **Blooms Taxonomy** (revised)
  David Krathwohl (2002) published a revised version of Blooms Taxonomy (1976), which can be used as a framework for instructional design. The revised version expands the table to two dimensions called knowledge dimension and cognitive dimension.
  Blloms Taxonomy is on one hand a very old theory but still offers some useful and state-of-the-art ideas as an impact to pedagogical work.
  Since the adaption of Krathwohl in 2002, the Taxonomy is useful for the definition of the taught competences. For example, the terms "understand", "analyse" and "evaluate" reflect parts of the competence model and can be used as typical key words in the definition of taught competences.

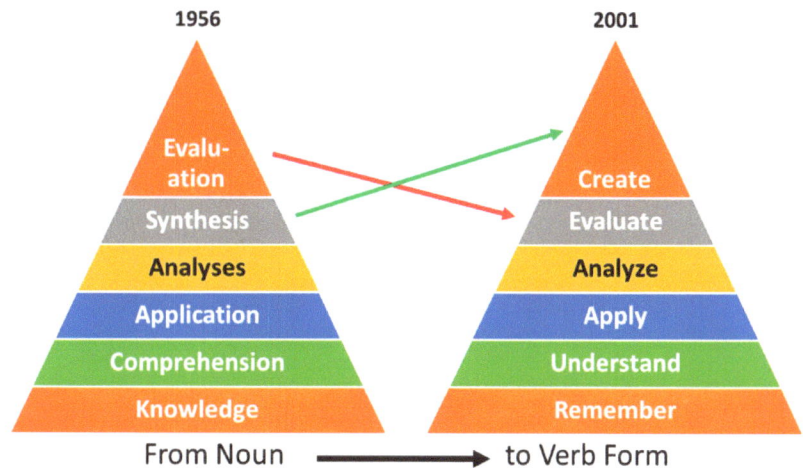

Figure 5: Blooms Taxonomy revised (after: Leslie Owen Wilson, 2013)

The table shows the two dimensions and how a learning objective can be classified.

		The Cognitive Process Dimension					
		Remember	Understand	Apply	Analyze	Evaluate	Create
The Knowledge Dimension	Factual Knowledge						
	Conceptional Knowledge						
	Procedural Knowledge						
	Metacognitive Knowledge						

Table 1: The two dimensions of the revised Bloom Taxonomy
(see: Krathwohl 2002)

The Taxonomy of Educational Objectives is a scheme for classifying educational goals, objectives, and, if applicable, standards.

This can be used as a guide line for the definition of competences (following the definition of competences by knowledge, skills and attitudes).

2.3 Learner-centered Access

The teacher is the center of teaching – and the students have to learn. They are involved in watching, making notes and listening. They work individually on assignments, sometimes they look to get help from other students. Cooperation is normally discouraged and felt as disturbing during lessons and lectures. This has been the situation for decades. Besides that, various accesses to teaching exist – in many cases with the origin in early age education like the Montessori approach.

In the fifties of the last century several theorists promoted a shifting from teacher centered learning to student centered learning. Here names appear like Jean Piaget, John Dewey or Carl Rogers.

The use of technology in teaching and the huge changes in society shifted the typical approach to teaching. Modern teaching is more focusing on the student in the center of the learning process (Felder 2010).

Here is an interesting statement of Tony Bates (2003, p 35) about learning:
Learning is seen essentially as a social process, requiring communication among learner, teacher and others. This social process cannot effectively be replaced by technology, although technology may facilitate it.

2.3.1 Origin of learner-centered teaching

The origin of the term is not clear. In the late 1980, Richard M. Felder shifted his professional focus from science teaching to the research and publication of aspects of teaching and learning. In his papers the expression of student-centered learning appears. He promotes to set a focus in teaching to active learning by involving students in relevant activities instead of ex-cathedra lectures as well as cooperative learning.

This approach finally led to the current idea of learner-centered teaching. This idea covers a wider range in education – students always are associated with university. Especially in Adult Education or Vocational Education and Training people coming from the working world are not used to sit and listen lectures – they want to learn, to practice and to be involved actively. Hands-on is a standard because this target group needs practical knowledge and skills for practical use in their profession.

This led to the shift from student-centered to learner-centered approach in teaching covering all people in a learning situation. School education – especially in upper classes – is still using very traditional teaching stiles very near to a teacher-centered access.

2.3.2 Characteristics of learner-centered teaching

Maryellen Weimer (2012) describes in her book the main characteristics of a learner-centered approach in teaching and mentions several advantages. The higher level of engagement of the students in the learning process is an important fact. More engagement normally means a higher level of learning outcomes. Being actively engaged in the learning process, students can develop sophisticated learning skills and control their learning as self-determining people.

The learner-centered access to teaching also teach the learners how to think, to learn how to solve problems, to analyze arguments, and evaluate evidence. All these items are soft skills and essential for effective learning. It is clear that learners do not pick up all these skills automatically – the teacher (trainer) has to lead and guide the learners so they can develop the requested skills. Once learned, these skills are useful for further learning.

Learner-centered teaching also encourages learners to act more critically in their learning. They reflect more on what they are learning and in the same way how they are learning. This results from the self-responsibility in active learning. Learners are not passive consumers anymore.

Furthermore, self-responsibility initiates some motivation because they feel responsible for their learning and they also feel that they have more control over their learning process. Teachers are not yet the only decision makers also learners are. They share responsibility with their students and therefore act more as a learning coach than the only person responsible for knowledge transfer (as it is still standard in teacher-centered learning).

Another positive effect is the shifting of the learner from the lonesome fighter to a valuable cooperator in learning for the classmates or other

learners in the attended course (educational environment). No doubt, that the teacher finally owns the expertise and the obligation to share, but learners well connected can learn from each other in a successful way.
Finally, teachers can also learn from the learners in a learner-centered environment – that is an additional amazing fact of that way of teaching.

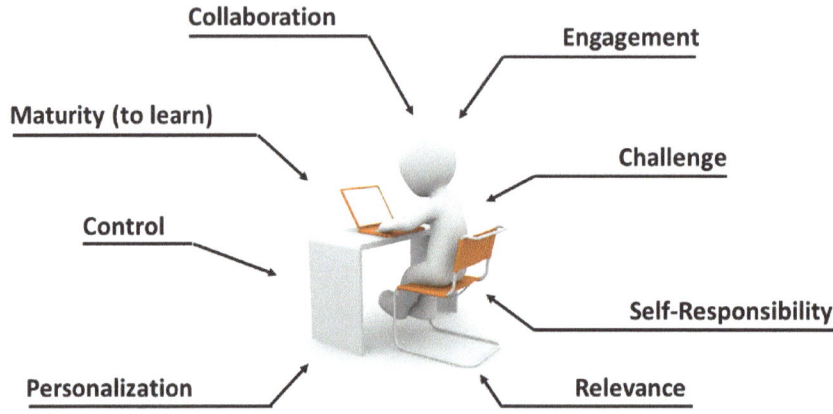

Figure 6: Learner in a learner-centered environment

2.4 Competence based learning outcomes

First, it is necessary to explain or define the various terms used in defining the goals of learning.

In literature three different terms are used to explain what the aim of a learning activity can be: objectives, competencies, and learning outcomes. A possible definition could be:

- **Objective**
  An objective is a very general statement about the larger goals of the course or program.
- **Learning Outcome**
  A learning outcome is a very specific statement that describes exactly what a student will be able to do in some measurable ways. A competency may have several specific learning outcomes so a course typically contains more outcomes than competencies.

- **Competency (or competence)**

    Competences are a general statement detailing the desired knowledge, skills, and attitudes (or behavior) of learners graduating from a course or program. Competences often contain several learning outcomes.

The Business Dictionary (2016) defines a competence as "A cluster of related abilities, commitments, knowledge, and skills that enable a person (or an organization) to act effectively in a job" or a specific situation.[9] The understanding and use of the term competence is not uniform in Europe. In various European countries competence oriented learning or competency based learning outcomes are used. An overview of different national approaches to the use of competences in learning and to define the learning goals by competence is available.

Competence-based learning (or competence-oriented learning)

This refers to systems of instruction, assessment, grading, and academic reporting that are based on students demonstrating that they have learned the knowledge and skills they are expected to learn as they progress through their education.

Standards

Standards are set up and established by an authority to provide a rule for the measurement of items like quantity, weight, extent, value or quality. Standards are often evaluated in standardized tests (as it's done for example in the K-12 education in the United States).

To define learning outcomes both competences and standards can be used.

2.4.1 What are competences?

Competences consist of three different elements: knowledge, skills and attitudes (or behavior). Each element is necessary but the weight can differ. For example, in language teaching the competence to use a specific vocabulary is focusing on the knowledge of the various words. The skill is to use them in the correct context depends on the knowledge (which is obviously dominant) and the attitude means the behavior in using the correct terms consequently.

---

[9] http://www.businessdictionary.com/definition/competence.html#ixzz3xzbqrtMq [14/12/2015]

In programming a computer, the knowledge of the specific language elements is clear, but the skills to create a well-working appropriate program fulfilling all requirements is the dominating part. The behavior could be to care automatically for all security features for example to avoid exploits in memory allocation (which will open the computer to hackers).

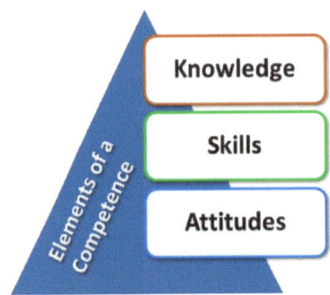

Figure 7: *Structure of a competence (see Mazohl 2015)*

The European Commission (2007) describes the eight key competences for Lifelong Learning in terms based on knowledge, skills and attitudes. In the document communication in the mother tongue, communication in foreign languages, mathematical competence and basic competences in science and technology, digital competence, learning to learn, social and civic competences, sense of initiative and entrepreneurship, and cultural awareness and expression. In the document, the Commission (2007, p 3) describes:

> *Key competences are those which all individuals need*
> *for personal fulfilment and development, active*
> *citizenship, social inclusion and employment.*

2.4.2 How to define competence based learning outcomes?

Competence based learning outcomes do not describe what the learner must know but what the learner is able to do after the learning process. In most cases the description starts with "the learner is able to …" followed by a description of the activity. "To be able to do something" implicates to have some knowledge, to have the skills to do what is requested and to show the behavior to act always in a similar situation.

Here is a simple example taken from English language training:
In the third person singular, the "s" is added to the verb.

The description of the competence could be:
The learner is able to use a verb correctly, especially in connection with the third person.

1. The necessary **knowledge** is the difference between verbs in the third person singular and the others. In the regular forms the "s" is simply added, the verb "run" is changed to "runs". The knowledge also covers irregular verbs like "have" which is used as "has" or "go" which converts to "goes".
2. The **skills** are to decide in which context the verb is used and to integrate the knowledge about regular and irregular forms in a text.
3. The **attitude** (or behavior) means that you use your knowledge and skills in your talking as well as your writing consequently.

Competences may include more than one knowledge item.

In any case, modern learning does not mean to gain simply a knowledge but to learn competences, which include – like a skin – the knowledge as well as the skills. In many cases the attitude is the smallest part in the competence because in many cases the learned knowledge and skills let learners act automatically in the requested behavior.

2.5 Use of Multimedia

Multimedia is an always present fact in our environment. Video, TV, smartphones, social networks, and other similar appearances dominate our daily life.

Multimedia is a reality in teaching. Simple school books contain texts combined with images and drawings and therefore are multimedia based content. A special role plays multimedia in the teaching with technology. In the area of cognitive skills, the use of various multimedia objects in a suitable educational framework may satisfy different learning needs (Naidu, 2003).

2.5.1 What is multimedia?

Multimedia is more than one concurrent presentation medium (for example, in internet or from a DVD). While still images are a different medium than text, multimedia is typically used to describe the combination of text, sound, images or motion video.

2.5.2 Multimedia and learning

Learning can be seen as information acquisition. Another access is to understand learning as knowledge construction. There is also the approach that learning is a way to gain competences. The three mentioned items describe - more or less - the expectations of the result of learning.

There are so many different options what learning can be. Nevertheless, there are concrete research results describing methods and instructional methods for successful learning. The findings often mention the use of multimedia as an appropriate way to successfully reach the provided learning goals.

People learn better from words and pictures than from words alone. Richard Mayer (2005) indicates that students learn better with multimedia. He defines multimedia instructional messages as a communication containing words and pictures intended to foster learning.

Yea-Ru Chuang (1999) mentions in his study significant different learning effects found in four different learning settings: a combination of animation and text, animation and voice, animation, text and voice, and finally a free choice version. People in the animation, text and voice group scored in the test environment significant higher than the others. Multimedia can stimulate more than one sense at a time, and in doing so, may be more attention-getting and attention-holding.

Using multimedia offers the learners to collect information through a method that addresses their imaginations and interests. For the teachers using multimedia combined with a sense of teaching provides a motivating access to teaching and is a promising teaching method.

2.6 Assessments and Grading

Assessment is an integral part of instruction, as it determines whether or not the goals of education are being met. Additional, assessments are an important tool for teachers also to get a feedback to their teaching activity. In formal education, assessment is often a compulsory issue in the teaching process to give the authorities the possibility of grading.

To avoid misunderstandings, the used terms are explained how they are meant in this book:

- **Assessment** means the act of making a judgement about the learning outcomes (normally measured in competences) by appropriate methods.
- **Grading** means the level of study which has been completed by a learner during a defined period of learning (for example a school year). Grading often is connected with marks, which often follow a national standard.

Jabbarifar (2009) summarizes the importance of assessment in the classroom using the teaching of the English language as an example.

2.6.1 Why are assessments necessary?

As an integral part of instruction assessments have a large scope of different functions in teaching.
Finally, assessment can contribute to grading and may affect the decision about advancement or instructional needs.

2.6.2 Different types of assessments

Based on time and purpose, different types of assessments are usual as part of instruction:

- **Formative assessment** offers diagnostic feedback to learners as to teachers. It should be done regularly in short intervals.
- **Summative assessment** provides a description of the level of fulfilment of learning activities, learning modules, courses or classes. This is used

as a method to evaluate the learners' success at the end of the learning process.
- **Evaluative assessment** cares for information to the teacher in context with activities done by the learners.
- **Educative assessment** is integrated in learning activities and builds learners' understanding about their own learning.

The assessments' results should not be graded. They describe the learners' success and finally the gained competences.

2.6.3 Difference between assessment and evaluation

Sometimes assessment and evaluation seems to be similar; this similarity can lead to confusion.

Assessment focuses on the learning, on the teaching and also on the outcomes. Assessment is an interactive process between the learners and the teaching organization and provides information about the learning and learning results of the learners. There should be an ongoing assessment to improve learning and to provide information to the teachers about the learning progress of students. Assessment assists students in improving their learning and study routine.

Evaluation focuses on grades and may include classroom components different from the course content, for examples teamwork, involvement in discussions or similar elements. Evaluation is a summative process, taking place at the final part of the course or learning.

The terms evaluation and assessment are two items which overlap and are sometimes used interchangeably. For present purposes, "assessment" is confined to student learning and "evaluation" to course design and teaching. In a near relation it can be seen that obviously each produced informs the other.

A good means to address evaluation and assessment correctly is a short sentence: Evaluation is to teaching as assessment is to learning.

2.6.4 Grading

Grading is the result of an evaluation of the learning outcomes. Grading must follow certain given standards, so it is possible to compare grades of different learners. Teachers often do not have the freedom to develop their own grading plan due to the given directives and standards.

Nevertheless, some considerations should be done by each teacher responsible for grades given to students as a result of some teaching.

At the beginning, there is the meaning of each grade symbol in context of the given standards. In the standards, a clear definition must be available describing which objectives of the teaching results are evaluated and how – this is put as a summary into grades.

Grading includes several serious problems that are in discussion for many decades: Grades have to follow (traditional) rules and standards, grades often are subjective (given from the point of view of the teacher), in many cases meaningless or unrealistic. Often traditional grades do not consider the needs of the 21st century learners. All that problems must be taken into account in modern teaching.

Evaluation of learners is always summative. The evaluation can use the results of assessments and conclude them to a grade.

Walvoord (2010) offers in her book "Assessment clear and simple" various ideas and concepts for assessment and grading. In the used test environment for the current book, the guidelines and definitions of the school and the Austrian education system have been taken for the grading of the students.

2.6.5 Purpose of grading

Grades have a multiple role in teaching. They serve as an evaluation of student's work (following the defined standards). They also are a means of communicating to students and their parents, but also for future education or to future employers. They describe (more or less) the performance in education and the student's potential for further success. They also can be a source of motivation (as well as a source of frustration) for students.

Therefore, it is important that grades reflect the quality of student work precisely and student work is graded fairly and seriously.

2.7 Evaluation of Courses

The MIT Teaching and Learning Laboratory (2015) defines Evaluation

> **Evaluation** *is a judgment by the instructor or educational researcher about whether the program or instruction has met its Intended Learning Outcomes[10] (ILO).*

Evaluation of the courses itself is necessary on several levels (some selected examples are listed below):
- To measure the learner's success to gain the requested competences
- To measure the teaching quality of teachers and trainers
- To measure the institutional quality (for example in supporting the learners in their learning effort)
- To evaluate the course structure (instructional design, efficiency of the course) to create data for a continuous quality enhancement process.

2.7.1 Kirkpatrick's 4 Levels of Training Evaluation

The Kirkpatrick Four-Level Training Evaluation Model (2016) can be useful for trainers or teachers to measure the effectiveness of their training. The four levels are:

Level 1 – Reaction

This level measures how students reacted to the training. The measurement of reactions helps to understand how the training was received by the students (in the same way it helps to improve the teaching for the future).

Level 2 – Learning

At that level, you measure what your students have learned. At which level the competences of the learners increased (in many cases you will see knowledge at this point – but knowledge is only one element of a competence).

---

[10] The term intended learning outcomes is from Biggs, J and Tang, C. (2011): Teaching for Quality Learning at University, (McGraw-Hill and Open University Press, Maidenhead)

Level 3 – Behavior

At this level the change in the behavior of the students – based on the teaching - is measured.

Level 4 – Results

At this level, the training results are analyzed, especially the learning outcomes (or intended learning outcomes) as they were defined prior to the teaching.

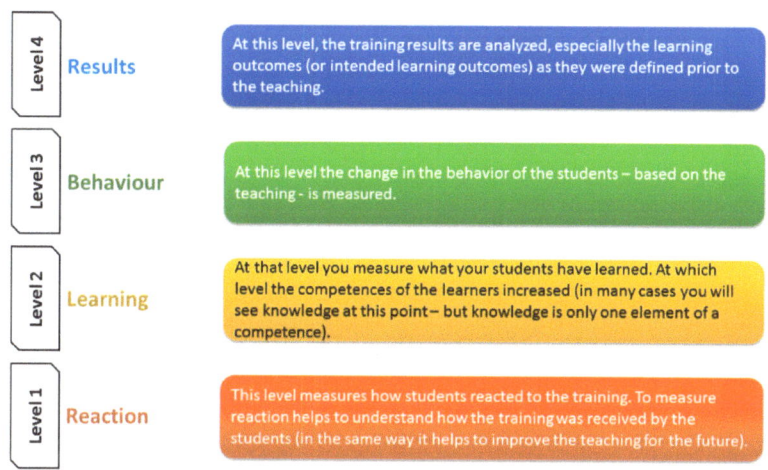

Figure 8: *The Kirkpatrick 4-Level Model*

To deepen in the Kirkpatrick Model, you may check the Kirkpatrick Partners webpage[11] or take a course.

Elements of the Kirkpatrick Model were taken for the formative evaluation of the teaching.

2.7.2 Self-Assessment of teachers

Self-assessment of teachers involved in the teaching process is an inevitable aspect of successful formative assessment.

---

[11] http://www.kirkpatrickpartners.com/OurPhilosophy/TheKirkpatrickModel [03/02/20169]

In a review of peer and self-assessment, Mills and Glover (2006) use Boud's (1991) definition of self-assessment as:

> *...the involvement of students in identifying standards and/or criteria to apply to their work, and making judgements about the extent to which they have met these criteria and standards.*

This method can be used to evaluate a course by the involved teachers. For self-assessment, several tools which can be used for the evaluation process exist.

Questionnaires

You should create a list of important items for your teaching success. After the end of teaching you try to fill out this list. Here a Likert scale[12] helps.

Reflection

Reflecting your activities and teaching behavior enables you to measure your teaching quality and the resulting success level. This also can be done by check lists with relevant questions like "How often did I involve students actively in the teaching", "Did I always use the optimized infra-structure in my teaching" and other related questions. In the case of reflection an evaluation using a Likert scale is useful.

In self-assessment, the biggest problem is the difference between self-perception and the perception of other people.

---

[12] Likert measures attitudes or opinions on a subjective way using a linear scale.

3 Learning and Teaching Environment

Technology enhanced teaching needs a special setting, teaching environment, and technical equipment. Two different options exist:

- The school provides the technical equipment for the students. This requires a personal computer for each student. The school provides the complete infrastructure including software and the devices. This setting is unrealistic due to the high costs and the necessary maintenance.
- Each student is responsible for their own equipment, including the technical device with the software. The school cares for the additional necessary infrastructure.
  Students' parents finance the necessary software using special educational offers of the software companies (for example educational licenses from Microsoft®).

This chapter describes the complete learning environment including the necessary classroom structure and other related issues.

Standardization of technical systems, like the access to networks using WiFi connectivity or cloud based tools, enables students easily to use their own devices. Gordon (2014, p 16) mentions the "familiarity with the interfaces and the software" as a benefit for students. On the other hand, Ackermann (2013) mention problems by bringing your own device.

3.1 Necessary Infrastructure

The school has to provide an infrastructure at real and virtual levels. This covers the classroom as well as the necessary equipment and tools.

3.1.1 Real level

The emphasis is laid on the well-equipped class rooms. The school has to provide the electrical supplement for the used hardware. This means an electrical plug for each student with the necessary power supply lines in several separated circuits. For approximately 25 students 3 different electrical circuits are necessary.

Another issue is the placement of the power plugs. They must be placed at the students' tables to avoid incidents by the exposed wires.

Each classroom needs a projector with the option to plug the teacher's laptop or with a fix installed personal computer. The requirement to the projector is relatively high. It should be a 16:9 format with a screen width of approximately 3 m to 4 m (to supply students best sitting in a distance of 6 m to 8 m). The projector must be strong enough to be used at daylight so that the students can work in natural light environment.

3.1.2 Virtual level

The students must be supplied with a powerful network. The network can be accessed by wires, but to use WLAN (WiFi based) seems to be the better solution. The WLAN must be strong enough and must supply the necessary bandwidth to provide the students with the necessary data and enable those streaming videos.

A central accessible LAN drive foreseen to provide material for the students may be an advantage, but is not a must. The distribution of the material is also possible using a learning platform or some cloud based storage if the necessary bandwidth to the Internet is available.

3.1.3 Occurring problems

The permanent access to the Internet gives the students the possibility to use services, web 2.0 applications or the learning platform during the lessons.

Nevertheless, the access to Facebook, Instagram or other social networks is available – and students will use them during the lessons as well. This leads to a distraction and must be considered in planning the infrastructure or the lessons.

3.2 Students' Equipment

Students have to use their own devices. In this document these devices are addressed as laptops, notebooks or multiple devices. In general, multiple devices are possible and allowed. Also smartphones are in the group of multiple devices, from generation to generation smartphones increase the display size and approach the format of small tablets.

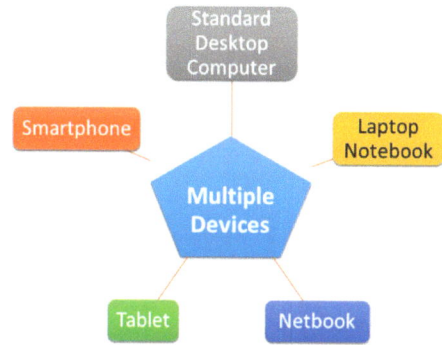

Figure 9: *Different types of multiple devices*

The findings of the students in practical work identified several problems with tablets and smartphones, especially in taking notes in class.

3.2.1 Keyboard

Students found out that using tablets without an appropriate keyboard prevents to take notes properly. A second issue is the fact that without a well-fitting keyboard ten finger blind writing is impossible and typing is extremely time consuming. Additional the build-in keyboards (visible at the display of the device) do not support all characters, especially from Greek language or mathematical signs.

3.2.2 Software

A second problem is the software. Especially smartphones but also tablets use apps. These type of software does not provide all necessary properties. Currently Microsoft® offers a cloud-based version of word, which can be used for free, but does not support all features which are suitable for the students.

Another issue is the delivering of content, for examples animations and simulations which are exclusively available in a Windows® format as an executable file. These products cannot be displayed on multiple devices.

3.2.3 Operating system

The operating system of the used devices also plays a role. Here the majority of the students uses Windows (in various versions), but Apple systems are used as well. An absolute minority uses Linux-based operating systems and in this group the most problems arise. Using word processing software like Libre Office makes it possible to use the provided material easily, a problem arises, like mentioned above, using the special simulations and animations.

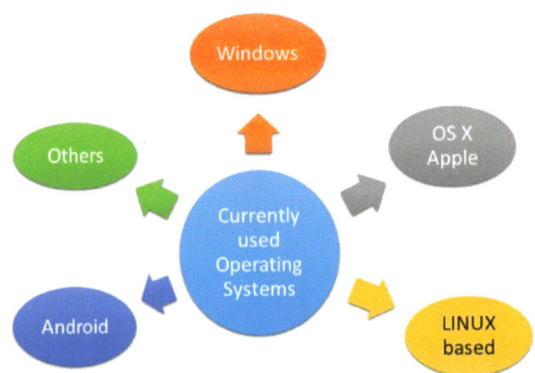

Figure 10: Operating Systems used by the Students

3.3 Students Pre-Knowledge

Student have to be able to master their tools. This covers the use of their devices as well as the necessary competence to use the software. Additional they have to bring the knowledge how to organize the data and their notes with them. This includes the primary work during class as well as the management of data, the organization of the notes and the necessary backup strategy.

3.3.1 ICT knowledge

The students have to own specific ICT-knowledge which must cover the following listed competencies:

- Be able to use word processing at an advanced level to take notes at an adequate level
- Be able to work with images and graphics, especially to produce and process the various multimedia elements for the notes
- Be able to work with spread sheet programs and simple mathematical tools to create simple calculations and statistics, for example to evaluate the results of their hands-on experiments.
- Be able to handle the file management in the frame of the used operating system to organize their data and notes physically.
- Be able to use archive files, like the classic ZIP format.

The communication competences focus on the data exchange, the access to the learning platform and the upload of assignments (for example protocols of hands-on activities).

3.3.2 To know how to organize learning

The biggest challenge for the students is to organize their learning. In the same way as the teacher provides well-structured material during class the students must bring the necessary competences with them to know what to do with the material, how to use it for reflections, or how to prepare themselves for competency checks. All the mentioned competences must be learned before the technology enhanced teaching starts.

For example, it seems to be useful to practice how to take notes in lessons teaching the mother tongue. This should be done in an early stage of the students' learning, maybe during the time the students pass in secondary school. To start in upper secondary school is obviously too late.

The organization of the learning is a long lasting learning process and could be combined with the teaching of ICT knowledge. In both fields students need to organize data and material in a systematic way using IT competences. To learn how to learn is a long lasting, sophisticated process and must be taught to the students in various subjects at faculty level. It should be part of the quality management of a school that the teachers involved in lessons in secondary school teach the pupils in their subjects how to manage their learning. The mentioned teachers must be educated in learning theory of the affected age group of pupils as well as on faculty level the continuous education of teachers must be kept at the state of the art.

Rozman & Koren (2013) mention the competences students have to have for successful learning, based on the definitions of the European communities. As a result, the study names five essential learning goals, highlighted by the students: a broader view on knowledge, the ability to acquire knowledge, the ability to transfer knowledge, the ability to transfer theory into practice, and a good knowledge of methodology. In the same document they discuss the student's goals, desired learning outcomes and skills to achieve their learning goals.

The European Communities define (in the frame of the eight key competences) the necessary competences students have to develop:

- learn autonomously,
- be self-disciplined,
- work collaboratively,
- share what they have learnt,
- organize their own learning,
- evaluate their own work,
- seek advice, information and support when appropriate

Hofmann (2008, p 173) describes the term learning to learn as the most important and vital for people trying to deal with the world that is changing rapidly. It should be clear that the teaching of the mentioned competences is essential for the further success of the students in their learning.

Hoskins & Fredriksson (2008) describe the process of learning to learn including measuring methods based on the key competences defined by the European Commission.

3.3.3 Access to the learning platform

The use of a learning platform is not a mandatory issue in the discussed teaching method but facilitates the teaching for teachers as well as the learning of the students. The platform offers the students a central access point, as they can find the repository with all materials in this platform, in which they can also perform the competence checks. A web based platform enables the access from anywhere at any time.

Students must know this platform, especially how to access and how to use the necessary items like repository, download of material and participate at an electronic competence check.

The competence of using an appropriate eLearning platform must be available from the beginning of the teaching.

3.3.4 Other pre-knowledge

Students should bring some practical experience in handling simple experiments in the hands-on sessions. This means some manual dexterity to perform the experiments, to do the precise measurements, to collect data and to watch precisely what happens.

For hands-on activities it is also necessary to know how measured values are noted, processed, evaluated, and interpreted. The most important and mainly used tool will be Excel to create the tables from the measured data. To know typewriting is an essential skill for participating in class efficiently. The best precondition is that the students know the ten fingers blind writing system and are practiced to use it permanently and to type with a high speed (which means more than 100 correctly set types in the minute).

3.4 Learning Platform

A central learning platform enables the students to access material easily from everywhere at any time. This implies a web-based eLearning platform which must be password protected for the students to secure their privacy. An eLearning platform is a tool to distribute or provide content or material. Nevertheless, it supports the teacher as a pedagogical tool in active teaching.

Finally, the platform supplements the teaching process by providing the basic materials used in class as well as providing additional material for the students. This material is a kind of help for students to reach the learning goals and to prepare themselves to competence tests or other assignment activities. The performed electronical competence can be used for the formative evaluation.

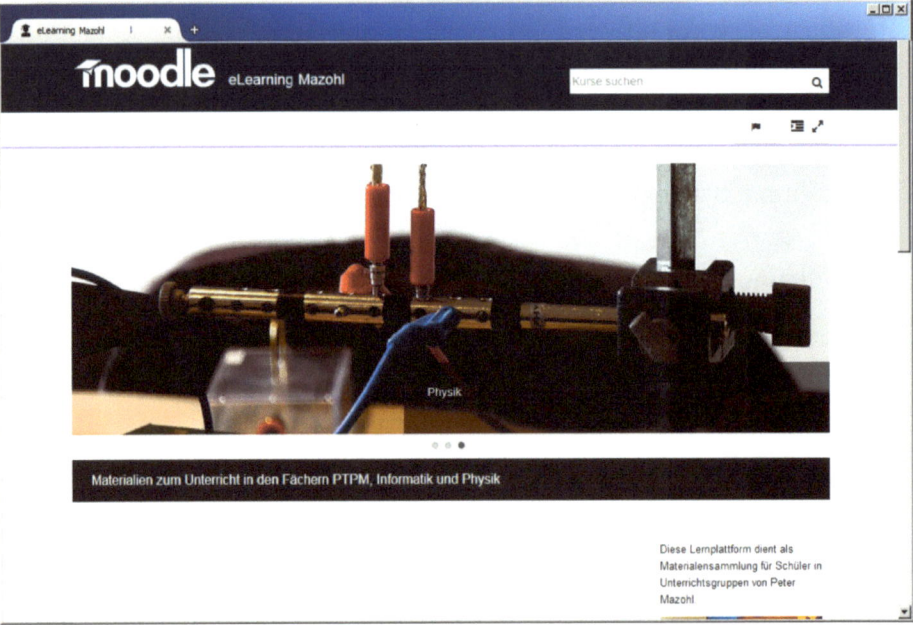

Image 1: *Screenshot of the used eLearning platform (Moodle 3.X)*

3.4.1 Provided features of the platform

A well-fitting eLearning platform offers a set of helpful features and tools to the teacher.

- **Repositories**
  The platform should supply repositories to distribute material like the core texts and graphics used in the various chapters.
- **Forums - Communication**
  Forums can be used as a central information tool or for cooperative or active learning. In the last time, the use of Facebook is intensively

discussed, but the study of Tzimopoulos (2015) proved, that students appreciate the use of only one central learning platform and that the majority of them does not like several tools distributed as Web 2.0 tools in the internet.

A second problem is the missing experience in using Facebook as a communication tool, here significant scientific studies clearing the effective use, the quality in teaching or the effectiveness are missing. The same considerations are valid for WhatsApp groups which became very popular at school within the last years (starting approximately from the year 2010).

- **Competence check**

  The competence test created to test the learning progress of the students can be performed easily using the eLearning platform during the school year. These formative assessments can be evaluated easily using the grading methods implemented in the eLearning platform or adopting them to specific environmental conditions in school.

  As an alternative, the teacher could use electronic interactive PDF documents, which the students have to check for facts (in closed questions) or to answer open questions.

- **Upload space for students**

  The platform can be used to upload the results of group works additional to presentations during class. Using this the material is continuously available for all students. Moreover, it can be evaluated by the teacher easily.

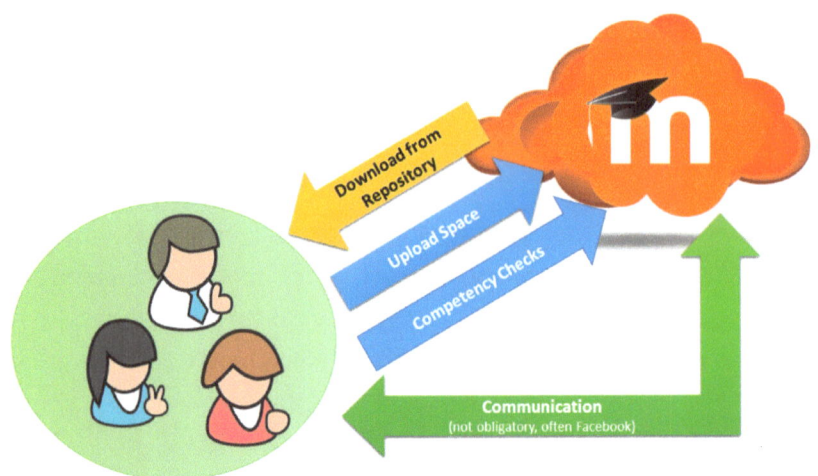

Figure 11: Possible use of the eLearning Platform

3.4.2 Needs of students

For the students, an easy and simple way must be prepared and foreseen to access the learning platform. The graphical design of the learning platform must supply multiple devices. It must be possible to access the platform from a laptop (using the currently wide spread screen format of 1366 x 768 pixels) or, as the extreme different technic, from a smartphone. This means to use a strict responsive design for the learning platform. So students may access the content using their multiple device to check forums, to quickly check content or to post something in a forum independently from where they are and which device is available.

As a result from the focus groups, an interesting fact is that students do not use their smartphones for "real" learning but to check news, assignments, the availability of content or post maximally a short message in a forum. Learning using the platform is mainly done on the laptop, because there a standard keyboard is available for writing (or taking notes), as it is needed for the various activities. This means that writing on a keyboard is an essential need of the students in learning and should not be underestimated.

3.4.3 Contribution to students' learning

Students' ability and attitude are success factors in reaching the learning goals, the existence of an eLearning platform only supports them in their doing. If students decline to use the platform, learning is reduced to the traditional onsite class and the additional effort of the students in reflecting or mental summarizing what they have heard during class. The eLearning platform is an option to do more than the minimum of effort, it is a chance for students to use it if they have missed something during class or because they have got ill or missed lessons due to other reasons.

It is in the responsibility of the students to use more than the basic material distributed to them. The eLearning platform can be used, but must not.

A change of the teaching system to Blended Learning would set the eLearning platform to a higher level of importance. Not the eLearning platform itself, but the motivation of the student to use it and to create some personal benefit in their learning contributes to the students' learning. The intention of the main use of the platform was to offer a repository for the students, provide sometimes joint and collaborative students' activities and to use the assessment tools for the competence tests.

3.5 Classroom and Labs

The typical classroom for ex-cathedra teaching consists of a teacher's desk opposite of the students' desks. A blackboard (or a whiteboard) is used by the teacher to make notes, students take notes by handwriting using exercise books. Sometimes as a technical equipment a computer with a projector is available to present multimedia content.

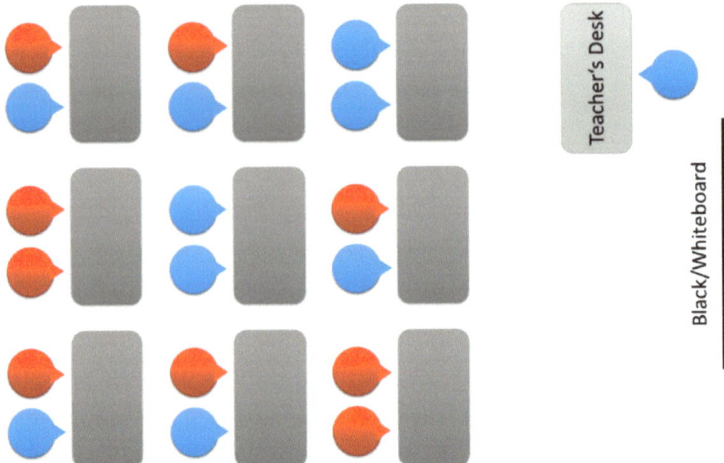

Figure 12: Typical classroom in onsite teaching (ex-cathedra teaching)

3.5.1 Minimum classroom for technical enhanced teaching

It is easy to change the classroom described above to a fitting environment for technology enhanced teaching. It needs a projector with a suitable projection screen and a computer to display the presentations. The room must offer power supply for the multiple devices of students and the students have to care for their access to the Internet.

3.5.2 Classroom for learner-centered teaching

A classroom for learner-centered teaching should provide a different setting. Nevertheless, students must have free view to the projection screen, but on the other hand the facilities for cooperative activities must be available. This is to support team-based assignments during lessons, as well as partner work.

The desks must provide enough space to place a laptop beneath other material, books and tools. Electric plugs must be available due to the limited battery life of common laptops.

Students must have free sight to the projection (or maybe a SMART board is used).

Especially for partner work an option must be foreseen to build groups, for example around a table, to analyze special issues, to answer questions, prepare presentations, or simply to create material as the result of an assignment.

The classroom should provide the option for the students to print texts or documents. Even in the digital area, paper is still needed in the learning or working process.

With well-fitting furniture, it is easy to switch from the typical classroom to a group learning situation during class. All-purpose or versatile classrooms can be used for technology enhanced teaching easily.

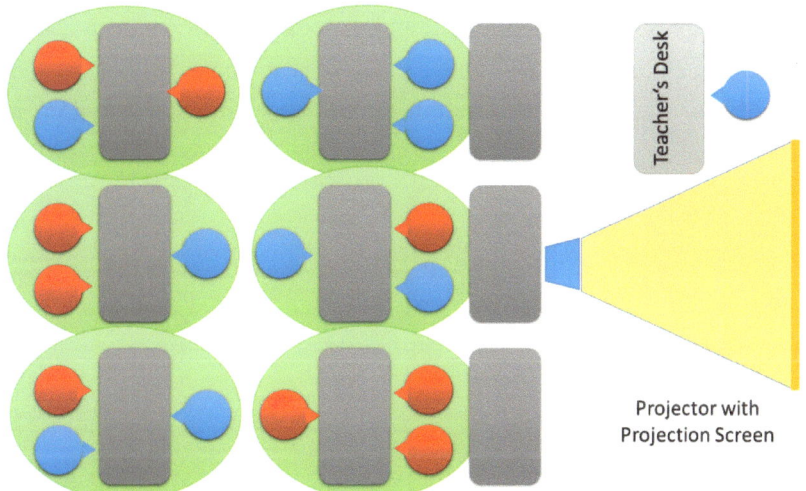

Figure 13: Versatile classroom

The standard classroom can be changed by splitting the students into groups of three working together as a small group (symbolized by the green oval). Turning back, they can report from the group results and continue to follow the presentations displayed at the screen.

This classroom must be supplied with an appropriate projector and the projecting facilities (connection for the teacher's laptop or fix installed computer).

3.5.3 Lab

The practical work in a lab situation increases the knowledge in physics as it enhances the skills of the students, especially in practical context. Special hands-on activities can create a deeper understanding of special matters as well as they care for better deepening of the learned and practices context. Standard and essential experiments should have been done by the students during class (if possible).

Hands-on activities should be performed in small groups of three. The group size of three results from the research of Laughlin et alt. (2006, p 649). The findings demonstrate, that groups perform better than single individuals. If the group size is too big the performance also decreases. A group size of three seems to perform best. The obvious reason can be found that individuals or groups of two are too small to care for a broad impact, bigger groups are more confusing or contain members are not contributing to work.

4 Teaching Experience

4.1 The Teaching Method

The presented teaching method is using a mix of a pedagogical framework, a special approach to the use of multiple devices, and a well-developed system for the assessment. All these items are in accordance of the teaching specifications for high schools in Austria. A transferability guide in chapter 7 provides ideas and descriptions for adapting the method for other subjects, in other fields of education or even in other countries.

The method uses a special, but common teaching environment, combined with a specific pedagogic approach and special tools.

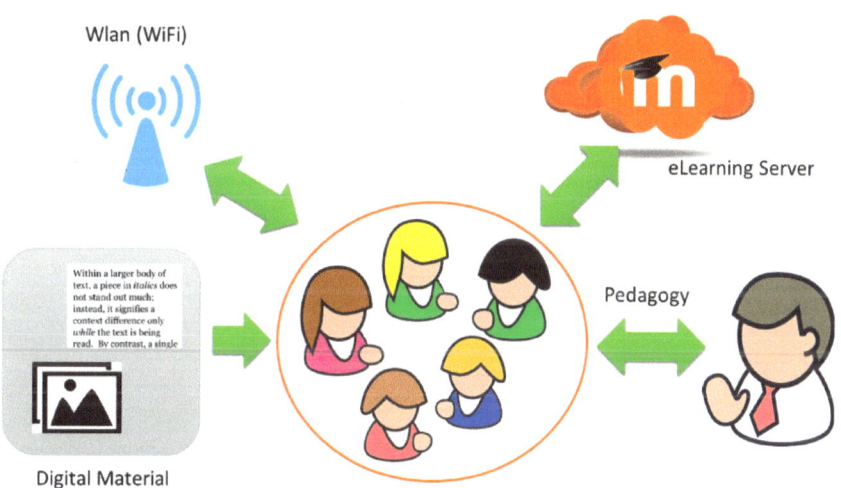

Figure 14: Teaching elements and items

The various items as displayed in the figure are identified and discussed in this chapter.

4.1.1 Digital material

Students have to take notes during lessons and are supported by the teacher by digital material for each chapter. A package consists of a basic text, a set of graphics and images, and sometimes of a simulation program or an interactive tool.

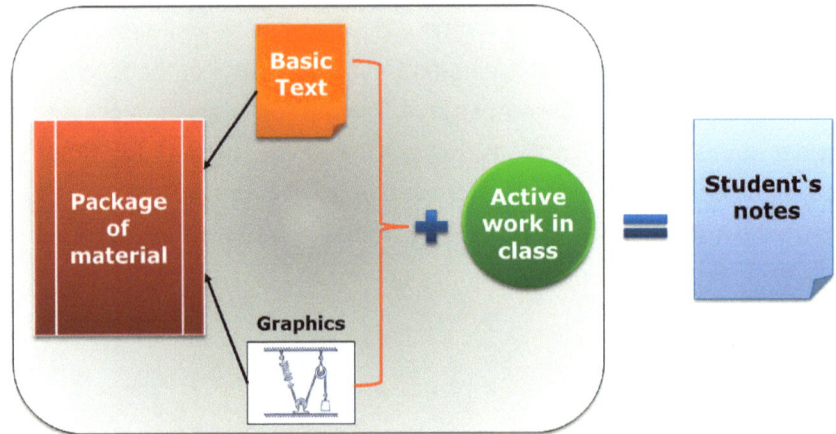

Figure 15: Material distributed to the students

4.1.2 Network connection

The school provides a WLan network so the students can connect with their multiple devices to the Internet easily. This network also provides a server based storage for each student (this is a benefit for the students but not necessary for the teaching). The access to the internet enables also the use of the eLearning platform (Moodle).

4.1.3 eLearning platform

For the eLearning platform, a web-based Moodle server is used. The system works as a repository and provides all the digital material well-organized in courses. Additional material is also available in these courses. The PowerPoint presentations used during class are also provided at the Moodle server, as they are converted into multimedia presentations. The Moodle server is used for competence checks.

The teaching method is performed in onsite teaching, therefore other features of the Moodle system are not used, like forums. The students meet face to face every day therefore it is easy for them to manage all communication at school.

4.1.4 Pedagogy

The pedagogical framework uses "the best of available pedagogy" taken from the theories summarized in chapter 2 of this book.

The framework covers the essentials of teaching based on a learner-centered approach as well as the activities during class and the assessment.

4.2 Preparation Work

The preparation work for lessons starts with the definitions of the taught competences. The descriptions of the competencies are taken from the curriculum. The various competences are put together to a learning unit, which is split into single lessons during the further procedure.

4.2.1 Definition of the competences

Figure 16: *Competences and integrated Key Competences (Source: Mazohl, 2016)*

As a source of the competences the curriculum for teaching physics in Austrian High Schools is taken. As an overlay, the eight key competences, as defined by the European Commission, are included.

The European Commission (2007, p. 3) considers these key competences "equally important, because each of them can contribute to a successful life in a knowledge society." The mentioned key competences are considered as necessary to master

> *"a whole new digital world, not only by acquiring technical skills, but also by gaining a deeper understanding of the opportunities, challenges and even ethical questions posed by new technologies"*
>
> *European Commission (2007, p. 3)*

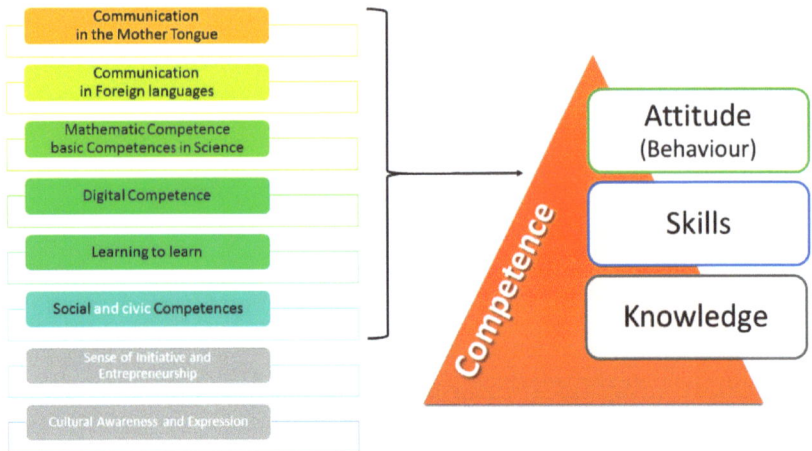

Nevertheless, not all of them are represented equally in the teaching process (due to the subject).

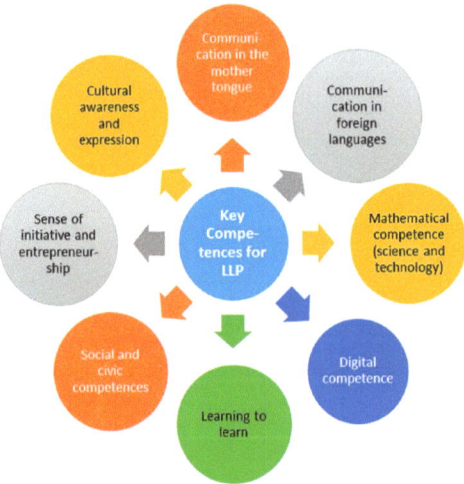

Figure 17: Key Competences, as defined from the European Commission (for the LLP Programme)

These key competences are integrated in the teaching process even if the students are not aware of it. Here are some examples, which show, how this is done:

- Communication **in the mother language** is standard in teaching (even if in Content and Language Integrated Learning CLIC a foreign language can be used). In Austria, we do not further use the expression "mother language" due to the high number of people with migration background but the term "spoken language" which means the language normally spoken in the family.

Students are taught to express and to interpret concepts, thoughts, feelings, facts and opinions in both oral and written form (listening, speaking, reading and writing), and to interact linguistically in an appropriate and creative way in a full range of societal and cultural contexts (European Commission 2007, p. 4). This is an issue especially in education and training.

During discussions or other verbal involvements students are regularly corrected in the case of errors, they are taught alternative terms as well as the related loanwords. Students are taught to use the correct technical terms as part of the terminology. Reading and the identification of key words in used texts are often performed, also in upper classes, to practice the understanding of content and the analyses of the context. To grasp meaning from reading is regularly executed in lessons.

- Use of **foreign language** is done during watching videos or using texts in a foreign language (exclusively English). The focus is set to the ability to understand spoken messages and to read and understand texts written in English language. The use of multimedia, especially of videos or simulations, is a proven approach to use a foreign language.
- Teaching physics, the use of mathematics is included more or less automatically. This covers to explain and to understand basic mathematical principles or processes as well as to be able to follow logical chains and arguments.

  Mathematical skills can be trained in other subjects as well, even if it is not as simple as in science teaching.
- In technology enhanced teaching, **digital competence** is as well a basic skill as it is practiced and enhanced during the lessons and self-paced working. Due to the definition of the European Commission (2017, p. 7), the teaching and learning process the uses computers to retrieve, assess, store, produce, present and exchange information, and to communicate and participate in collaborative networks via the Internet.

A crucial issue in this context is the work with the learn platform and the exchange of documents.

- **Learning to learn** is an important issue in secondary education and must be included and trained with students from the beginning of the teaching process. Students taught in a technological enhanced learning environment must be able to organise one's own learning, including through effective management of time and information from the beginning (European Commission 2007, p. 8). The permanent use of the computer (or multiple devices) forces students to an intensive knowledge management. They learn to gather information, to evaluate this information and to put it in context of the learned content (as part of a defined competence). The described teaching method fosters a problem-solving attitude which supports both the learning process itself and an individual's ability to handle obstacles. Together with social competences, learning to learn is also practiced in group work (even if the students often do not really like this).
- Discussions during lessons, with a focus on physical background of environmental problems or in working life, develop the **ability to communicate constructively** in different environments, to show tolerance, express and understand different viewpoints, to negotiate with the ability to create confidence, and to feel empathy.
- Sense of initiative and entrepreneurship is a side issue and is integrated in science teaching, but only rudimental. Here the presentation of technical development is taken in account as well as the development of products which have an intensive physical background and are successfully placed at the marked.
- Cultural awareness and expression stay in context with the development of technical progress and the influence in society, culture, national and international development.

These eight key competences are (more or less) permanently present and create a background network in teaching. In the foreground are the competences associated with the curriculum.

4.2.2 Competence based teaching

Following the guidelines of the curriculum, learning units are defined. These units contain an associated part of the curriculum called "chapters". For each chapter, the taught competence is specified.

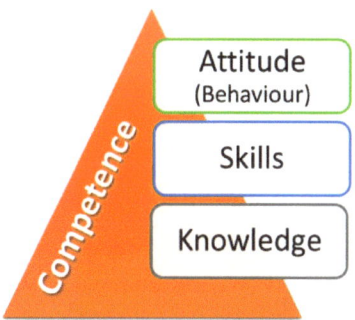

Figure 18: Competence description (Source: Mazohl, 2015)

Example "Current"

Here is an example for the chapter "Current and Electrical Current". A detailed description of a lesson is given in the following chapter 4.3.

The defined competence is to be able to realize current, to be able to measure and to explain the term current. Such a competence is split into the necessary knowledge, the skills which have to be developed by students and the connected behaviour.

- **Knowledge**
  Know the definition of the term current as a differential quotient
  Know the nature of current (based on moving charges)
  Know the measurement unit and know how to measure
  Know about dangerous settings
- **Skills**
  Identify situations where current is present and analyse the setting
  Be able to measure current
- **Attitude**
  Behave correctly in the various electrical settings
  Correctly use of current in the various settings

Knowledge	Skills	Attitude
• Know the definition of the term current as a differential quotient • Know the nature of current (based on moving charges) • Know the measurement unit and know how to measure • Know about dangerous settings	• Identify situations where current is present and analyse the setting • Be able to measure current	• Behave correctly in the various electrical settings • Correctly use of current in the various settings

Figure 19: Overview of the competence in the example

4.2.3   Preparation of the presentation

The preparation of a presentation is done by a mind map where all the necessary knowledge and skills related to the competences defined for the chapter are brought into a certain order. From this mind map the various slides of the presentation are created.

4.2.4   Preparation of the basic text file

For the presentation, a text file is created. This document contains the necessary descriptions of the taught content, including the related formulas and graphics and is used to create the presentation. Finally, the file is adapted to be distributed to the students for their notes.

The adapted text file is provided as a help for students to take notes. The file contains all necessary headings of the taught chapter in hierarchical order. Additional, in some cases parts of text of formulas which are difficult to create are yet available.

4.2.5   Preparation of lab experiments

As a next step, the experiments used for demonstration of taught content are structured and planned for practical realisation. These experiments are important to practice the ability to watch, realise and analyse processes and activities in context with the taught content. This strengthens the skills of the students to look through simple and also complex relations and physical structural conditions.

4.2.6 Selection of multimedia material

The preparation is completed by the selection of the requested multimedia material, mainly pictures and graphics for the students to complete the notes but also for the presentation. Videos and simulations are also selected and brought into an appropriate format to be used during class.

4.2.7 Finalization of the material

The complete data collection is used on one hand to create the PowerPoint® presentation and on the other hand to create the package of digital material provided for the students. This package is distributed to the students using the local network at school. The second way of distribution uses the eLearning platform Moodle. There the package is available from a repository. Additional, multimedia based material as well as the videos and the simulations are also available from a course provided at the eLearning platform.

4.3 Sample Chapter Creation

This chapter describes the practical development of a typical chapter as practiced in class. The sample focuses on the chapter "Current and Electrical Current". For this chapters several lessons are used for the presentations and various physical tests are foreseen.

It starts with the description of the competences taught in the lessons, the list is a derivate from the curriculum. The used methodology to teach these competences is oriented on settings from everyday life. The next step is to create the necessary mind map.

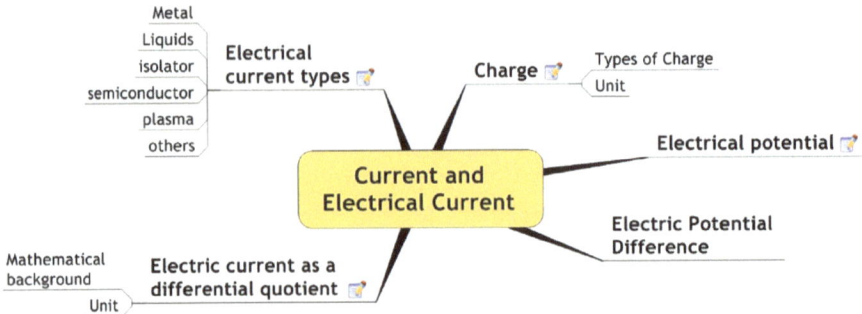

Figure 20: Mind map of the sample chapter

As described before, all the steps are executed and lead to the presentation and the package of material distributed to the students.

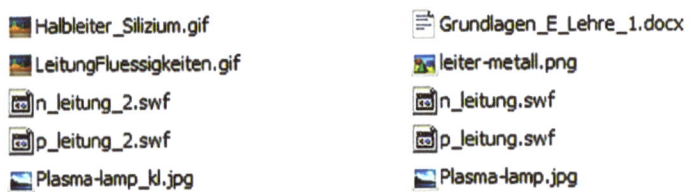

Figure 21: Content of the package of material distributed to students

The package's central item is the text document. Additional, the graphics are included. In this package two ShockWave® Files are provided as a simulation of the electric current mechanism found in semiconductors. These files can be watched in any browser providing a Flash® plugin.

The presentation is converted into a multimedia file, using the freeware tool "iSpring"[13]. This multimedia element is uploaded to the learning platform finally.

---

[13] iSpring is a free PowerPoint Converter. It adds an extra tab to the PowerPoint toolbar for access to all its functions. Further information is available at the webpage of iSpring Solutions https://www.ispringsolutions.com.

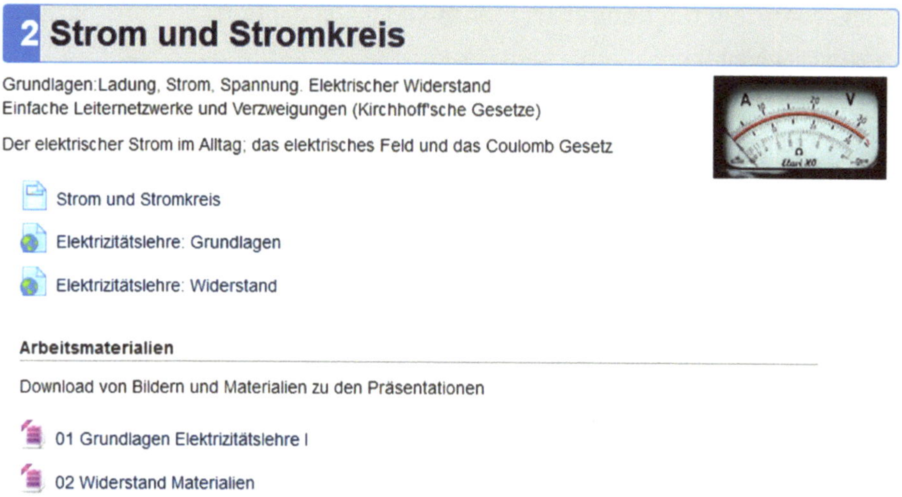

Figure 22: The described chapter in the eLearning platform

4.4 Students' Needs

Takahashi and others (2013) mention in the study about self-directed learning six groups of typical needs of students. They name time management, managing learning resources, the attitude and the learning environment as related issues. The study can be transferred partly to the described teaching method.

The approach to identify students' needs was using focus groups. A list, which shows how student needs were developed, was combined with the results of general student needs and taken as an impact from the mentioned study.

4.4.1 Focus groups

Three different focus groups with involved students were performed using the same question guides for all. Two additional focus groups with different students took place after the first session to evaluate the first round of focus groups. The students of the second session gave feedback to the foreseen open questions but were also confronted with the feedback from their colleagues from the prior focus rounds and could confirm the most of the feedback given there.

The question why they learn and what was their learning motivation was answered in a general way with the following listed items.

- Students want to create a long-lasting benefit for their personal future or to create the necessary knowledge as a basis of their further education.
  This means knowledge for life and the basis for lifelong learning. So many of the students proofed a certain status of maturity and vision for their future.
- Students need the final exams to be allowed to study.
  The most students are planning a further education either at a university or a university of applied studies and need the final exams as a kind of "entrance ticket" for further education.
- Many students confessed that they are interested in good marks (as a short-term issue), some of the students mentioned that grades are not so important and they do not have any ambition to appear as brilliant.
- Some students confess that they have fun in learning. This, unfortunately, was the minority of students.
- Some students learn because they have an impressing person as a teacher and like to follow the teachers experience and to benefit from their knowledge.
- The most students mentioned that multimedia content does not motivate them to learn.
- The students appreciate the simplest and most effective ways of learning.
- No student agreed to the idea that eLearning or the technology enhanced teaching will motivate them to learn more. They approach the method as "the natural way of modern learning" and want to increase their learning success in a simple way by using technology.
- In technology enhanced teaching the appropriate teaching and working environment is very important for them. They find the various occurring obstacles and technical problems like broken WLAN connection or not appropriate installed software or tools (these problems happen

regularly and cost time which could be used better by the students) annoying.

The mind map gives an overview of the selected items which are considered as the most important impact in the teaching process.

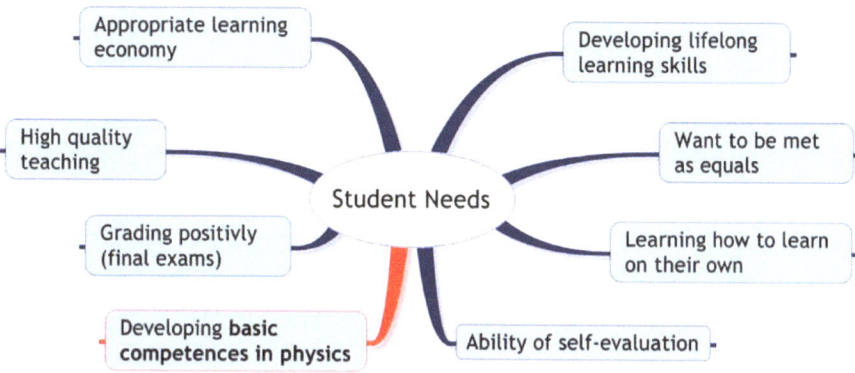

Figure 23: Students' need in the described learning situation

The listed needs can be categorized into two different classes from the point of view of the students.

4.4.2 Practical needs

The development of basic competences in physics is a typical practical aim. All students attended the classes on their own will, they have had finished the compulsory education and have selected this specific school type.
Identically, the positive grading of the class can be seen as a step towards positive final exams. This requires a high level of teaching quality and an appropriate learning economy. The learning economy means a time relevant approach to gain the expected competences and can be seen as a strategy to learn in short time the content and gain the related skills in an efficient way.

4.4.3 General needs

The second group covers the intention of the European Commission and is seen similarly by the students.

The most important mentioned item in the focus group with students (Mazohl, 2016) was the learning and teaching situation of the students. They want to be accepted by their teachers as adults; they want to be met as equals by their teachers (even if it is clear who will be the control device and the responsible person in charge), simply to meet them at eye level. In the focus group, some students mentioned that they feel treated as small kids from their teachers. This decreases their learning motivation and their impact and engagement to active learning. At that age, they are allowed to participate at elections or to drive a car. Therefore, they want to be accepted as partners in the learning process.

Other needs are the ability to learn, they have to develop and finally to use the competence to know how to learn, to be able to self-evaluate their learning and to increase their competences as well as to develop lifelong learning skills as a principle for current and further learning activities.

It is obvious that the needs more or less are in a close context of the described key competences.

4.5 Students' Involvement

The described teaching uses a learner-centered approach combined with traditional ex-cathedra teaching. The students and students' needs are in the focus of the teaching process.

These needs mentioned above give an impact to the designed students' involvement.

4.5.1 Presentation

During the lessons, students may watch a PowerPoint® presentation providing the basic information to the topic of the lesson. The PowerPoint presentations are kept simple and include a minimum text and often formulas or drawings, images or graphics.

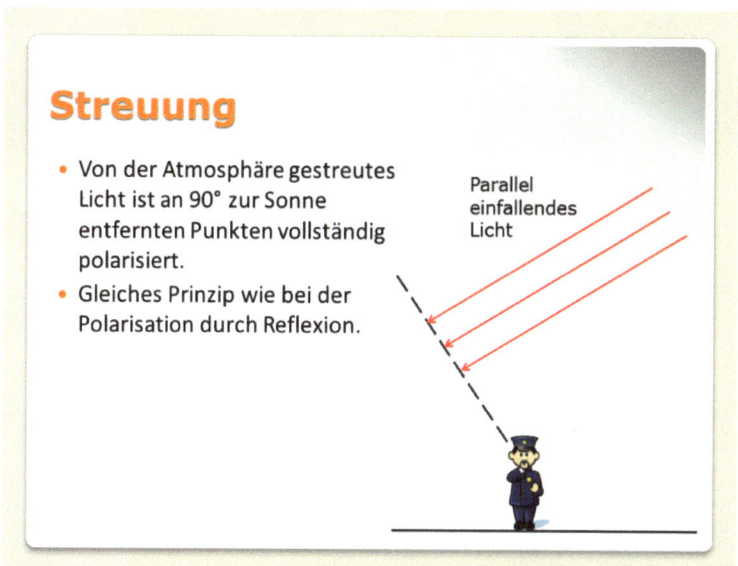

Figure 24: *Example of a presentation slide (polarisation of light, physics 7th form)*

Students follow the presentation and use the provided basic document to take notes, to summarize the content, to comment existing text, or to insert and place the provided graphics. Students are instructed not to copy the text of the presentation but to summarize the content using their own words in a way which is easy for them to reflect the content. This is in context to reinforce what they heard in the mind (Hawkins, 2010). These notes are crucial for the reflection of students (another aid is the uploaded presentations available at the eLearning platform). Personal notes are the best step for optimized retention and a successful reflection.

Image 2: *Students taking notes using their multiple devices*

During the presentation, the teacher poses competence oriented questions to involve the students actively. There questions may be answered by various students, the teacher evaluates the collected answers, explains correct results, explicates incorrect answers, and solves mistakes in thinking. Students should start such questions as well as giving an active impact to the understanding of the content, the related context, and the possible transfer to everyday life.

Another activity performed during the presentation is a reading exercise of crucial sentences for students. Here they must find out the key terms in context to the provided knowledge and to put these keywords into context of the current topic. This reading forces the students to grasp the meaning of reading and to develop an approach to analyses of texts and critical evaluation of the content and the provided information.

4.5.2 Discussion

During the lessons, discussions are started in the group of learners focusing on facts or conditions found in daily situations or common activities. These discussions are always moderated or chaired by the teacher. Results are summarized by the students and brought into a correct context of their notes. Hawkins (2010) mentions that discussion and debates reinforces learning. It creates clarity and understanding for the students. Listening to these discussions is as useful as rethinking the logical threads or to contribute with own ideas and thoughts.

Image 3: *Students contributing to discussions*

4.5.3 Group work

Group work is done regularly in various contexts. This can be a two-by-two joint problem solving activity with a short presentation or summary done by the group as well as practical involvement in lab experiments, assisting in physical tests, or other practical work.

The result of group work is either a personal experience and the development of skills or a presentation of the results of the joint work. In any case summing up notes must be taken by the students to own an appropriate material for the necessary reflection.

Group work often is performed as a typical hands-on experience, where the students can practice or try out special issues they have learned during lessons.

Image 4: Practical hands-on experiments performed by students

4.5.4 Additional Activities

Students watch regularly videos. As the students own their own digital devices the distribution of videos using the internal school net or the Internet is simple and quickly done. The students either analyse the video alone or in small groups of two or three. The videos are an impact for discussions or presentations of the findings. In any case, a summary of the findings must be given and put into correct context of the current topic.

For further reflections the students have to take notes of summaries and results of the interpretation of what they have seen or what they have been finding out.

4.6 Motivation

Richard Romando (2007) defines the term "motivation" in an appropriate way to explain motivation of students living in the digital age.

> *Motivation is defined as an internal drive that activates behavior and gives it direction. The term motivation theory is concerned with the processes that describe why and how human behavior is activated and directed.*

Motivation must be seen as a process and not as a product (Schunk, 2009 p. 4). This process must be put into context with specific needs of the involved person. The study of Lindner (1998) done in a vocational environment resulted in several motivation factors for employees. The first three were interesting work, good wages, and full appreciation of done work.

Motivational Factors

Motivation Factors for Employees	Motivation Factors for Students
Interesting work	Interesting Lessons
Good Wages	Good Results (or Grades)
Full Appreciation of Done Work	Full Appreciation of done work

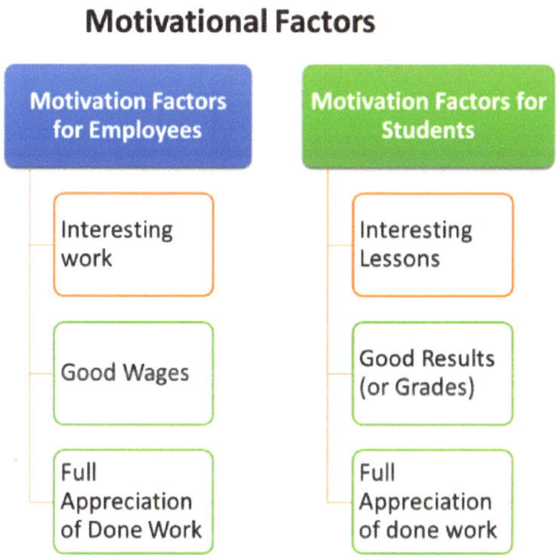

Figure 25: Comparison the motivation of employees and students

Fifteen years later, the factors may be shifted in the ranking, but are still relevant. The transfer from professional work to school from the first three items bring up (not in order)

- interesting lessons,

- good results (or grades) and
- full appreciation of work done.

To keep students interested in scientific topics may sound easy, but often missing understanding of complex interrelations disadvantages students and decreases motivation.

At school level (and in Higher Education as well) grades play an important role. Grades are deciding on further development, the access to the next educational level, and finally on the chances at the labour market. Ambition often is the source of the quest to gain high level grades. Sometimes also a kind of competition between students to grade better than others can be recognized. Nevertheless, at high school level grades are and will be an important factor for the motivation of students to follow the lessons intensively and to gain the foreseen competences.

The most interesting item is the "full appreciation of work done". In the focus group (Mazohl, 2016) students mention that they will meet their teachers at eye level and want to be accepted as equal partners doing a good job. This can be judged as the wish of the learners of a more cooperation based teaching behaviour of both students and teachers.

All these considerations were an impact in the discussed teaching method. The mentioned cooperative style is practiced intensively and results in a higher level of appreciation of the lessons and can be realized in the behaviour of students, who try to play a part in the lessons.

A critical item in all these considerations plays the maturity of the learners. In typical school environment, students basically attend the lessons on their free will (because they have finished the foreseen compulsory education) but there is the interest of their parents/family to attend school and to obtain a higher level of education as a fundament of better chances in the future.

Mazohl and Makl (2015) proofed, that the maturity of learners plays an important role in typical Blended Learning situations. As the age of the mentioned study addresses the same target group and sample it is obvious that the maturity of learners also plays a role in the motivation to learn using the presented teaching method.

4.7 Assessment

The Austrian school system provides several methods to assess learning and learning outcomes. Focusing on competences, the assessment used in the discussed teaching method focuses on an individual approach to evaluate the gained competences.

Individuals are evaluated as competent when they are able to consistently apply their knowledge and skills to the standard of performance (as required). The standards are described in the curriculum, but kept very open. This means that a precise description is missing and the teacher is required to evaluate the provided competence in a certain range of knowledge.

Assessment is the process of collecting evidence and making judgements on whether the competence has been achieved. Evidence of competences in general education usually is collected directly (by observation, oral questioning, or competence checks).

Assessment in learner-centered teaching should always be a formative process leading finally to the necessary grading or evaluation.

4.7.1 Continuous observation

Assessment cannot be an end activity. It is necessary for the teacher to assess the increase of competence to evaluate continuously the teaching process and teaching success as well as to watch students during their learning development. Carlson (2003) mentions continuous assessment as "listening closely to students, observing students as they are engaged in learning, as they are engaged with materials, and trying to understand what they understand." This can be done during lessons in the phases of active involvement, using the students' comments to examples or during discussions.

Continuous assessment is formative by nature. A key activity is the collecting of data, information and impressions about students' understanding. The techniques for continuous assessment used in the described teaching method are listening to conversations, purposeful questioning open questions, and the reactions, questions or contributions during the presentations or lab experiments.

4.7.2 Active involvement

Active involvement means to contribute to small case studies, to reflect facts and activities of daily life in the frame of the current learning content. Here the students have to develop the competencies to apply the gained knowledge and skills to explain facts, relations and dependencies.

Simple general knowledge has to be transferred into a scientific context and must be explained by the students using the currently and newly gained knowledge. That contains the analyses of formulas, mechanism or complex correlations as well as the simple describing of facts and processes.

4.7.3 Conversations, discussions and exams

These techniques are a type of embedded assessment with two stages of benefit. For the students, it is a possibility to proof their competences as well as to learn from conversations or discussions from others. For the teacher, it is a formative evaluation of the students' competences.

Oral exams are one-to-one discussions between the student and the teacher. The teacher uses special competence oriented verbs like explain, describe, put into relation and others to steer the discussion and to guide the student to use the gained competences during the discussion. The other students should follow the conversation between the student and the teacher and may contribute to the dialogue (this is recognized as part of an active involvement). All not directly involved students may be asked to special items during one-to-one discussions as well.

4.7.4 Web based competence checks

The eLearning platform Moodle offers a broad scope of testing options. Web based competence checks are performed regularly using these features.

An emphasis is laid on the use of multimedia elements like graphics or images. The various question types are used to offer different answering options like 4:1 answers, 4:X answers, cloze tests, selections or open answers.

Web based Competence Check

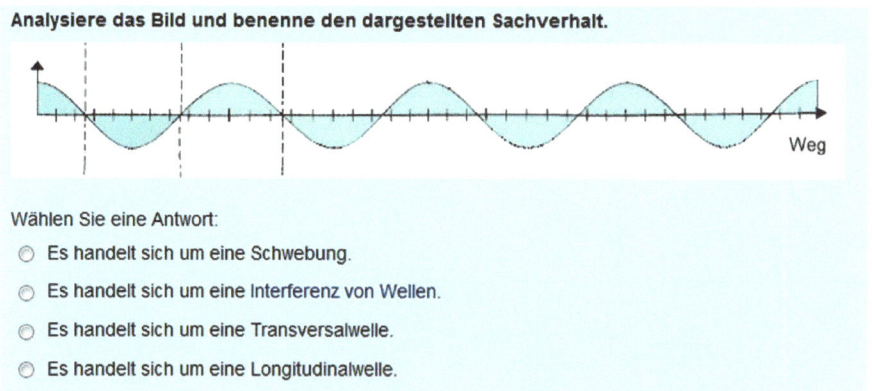

Figure 26: Example for a competence check question in the Moodle system (Physics, 7th form)

In the currently new version of Moodle 3.X the use of multimedia and the types of questions increased. Students are using intensively Web 2.0 tools and therefore are common with multimedia content. Therefore, it is necessary to keep the used tools at the multimedia level of the students and to care for a continuous development of multimedia based tools in Moodle, especially in the frame of tests.

Web based tests are evaluated automatically and impact to the grading as a puzzle piece comparable with observation and students' involvement.
External web based Web 2.0 applications or tools are not used except it is possible to integrate them into the eLearning system. The studies of Tzimopoulos (2015, p. 74) showed that learners want to have a centralized access to the learning platform and do not want to use a big number of different webpages neither for the learning nor for competence checks or anything else.

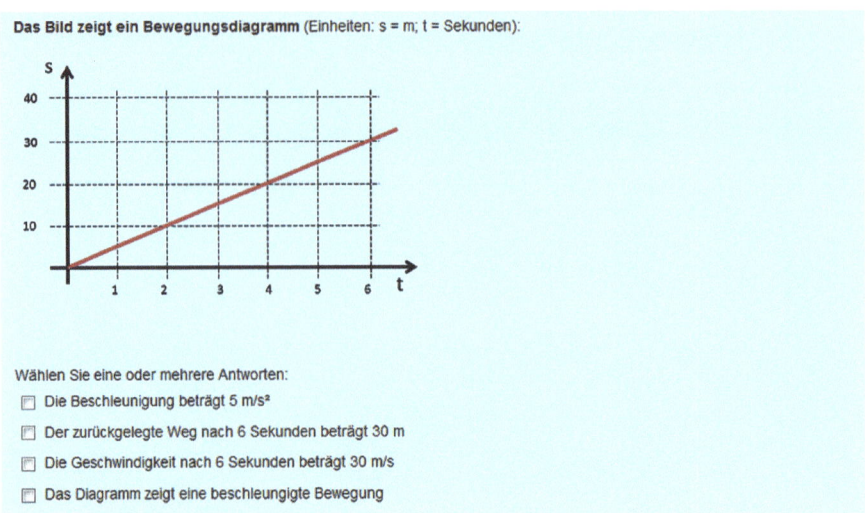

Figure 27: Example for a competence check question in the Moodle system (Physics, 6th form)

4.7.5 Grading

The process of grading requires teachers to make several decisions that are grounded in their personal value system in relation to the preconditions given by the school authority. Without doubt, the evaluation of gained competences is a continuous process which finally leads to grades. The system of assessing the new competences and how the final grades are calculated from the intermediate results is published and discussed at the beginning of each school year and agreed between students and the teacher.

Grading in Austria is based on legal advices from the school authority and the related law as well. Teachers have the freedom to use the range of given instructions to agree with their students individual grading procedures in the given levels and regulations.

Grades must be published in an intermediate report and for the school certificate at the end of the year.

Grades are discussed with the students four times during year and agreed jointly for the final school certificate. On their own wish students can volunteer to better the grades by doing an oral exam.

4.8 Results

The described teaching method was developed in a Grundtvig Learning Partnership in the frame of an LLP project. The approach from the Adult Education Sector got a special impact through the partner University of Limassol (Cyprus). In 2010 the method was transferred to school education and continuously enhanced and amended.

The first evaluation took place in summer 2010 and led to several changes and corrections. The grade of satisfaction was very high in 2010 and a case study performed during the evaluation process prove a high level of acceptance and appreciation of the teaching by the students.

In 2012, the shift to completely competence based teaching was carried out. Since that, the curriculum is split into chapters, a list exists of competences taught in class for each chapter. These lists are basis for the assessment in the final exams.

4.8.1 Concentration to basic competences

The current teaching covers the described chapters, topics and competences and builds the basic course with the essential knowledge of physics (as described in the curriculum) inside. This ensures a constant level of physical knowledge for each year.

4.8.2 Use of the eLearning platform

The eLearning platform is a kind of extension in this teaching method. Students can use it for their learning, but must not do so. All material is distributed to students by the internal WLAN and the workgroup server at school. Nevertheless, the platform offers benefits in various ways.

- Repository of the used material
  All texts, graphics and other multimedia based resources are made available by the platform
- Additional material is provided at the platform
  This can be used to enhance the teaching method to Blended Learning. In pure onsite teaching this is not a currently discussed option.

- Community tools of the platform are not used currently as the students are attending school five days the week, they meet each other daily and have the option to ask a teacher also every day.

A learning platform like Moodle is necessary if the school does not supply the students with their own user drives at school or if any central storage at school is missing. In this case, the best solution is an eLearning server accessible by the Internet. This implies a high level of knowledge of the teacher in context with Moodle or forces an institutional service. Following the research from Tzimopoulos and Filioglou (2015), other centralized repository solutions are an option as well. Web based facilities split on several cloud based places are no promising solution and negotiated by the students.

4.8.3 Students' satisfaction

The discussed method is well accepted by the students and produces good results, especially in comparison with other methods. Technology enhanced teaching needs strict and practicable concepts which can be executed by the students in a simple way. Students see the technology as a help for their learning and want to use it in an efficient way. They expect that technology makes learning more simple and time economically.

On the other hand, students identify missing preparation for technology based learning as an obstacle. This problem is a typical faculty problem and must be solved on that level. A promising approach is to teach the students how to take notes efficiently and completely at an early stage – maybe before the technology enhanced lessons start.

4.8.4 Teacher's satisfaction

The satisfaction of the teacher is ambivalent. The good learning results of the students demonstrate the suitability of the discussed teaching method. The feedback given by the students also can be evaluated as a positive sign. A special item is the time balance comparing traditional teaching with technology enhanced teaching. For example, the electronic competency checks produce extra work, but only once in the creation phase. After that, they are useful and efficient tools for the formative evaluation. Without doubt, the teachers using Moodle for the competence checks have to meet high demands. They have to invest some time in the learning of Moodle and they also have to spend regularly time for continuous training in the platform. From a practical point of view, the shifting from traditional teaching to technology enhanced teaching is in some way time consuming, but a must for modern teachers. Teachers are guides for students, setting examples of modern learning and using the current technical means efficiently. They should teach at a state of the art level and integrate technology in a convenient and efficient way. Therefore, the time factor should not play any role in considerations for teachers.

Another item is the difference between theory and real life. In the theory you learn about promising methods like learner-centered teaching or active teaching. In the reality, you teach tired students, which are exhausted from the just passed three hours' test and who are not really interested in contributing actively to class. This extreme example does not happen every day, but students in reality differ from the idealistic theory of modern teaching. This makes it difficult for teachers to meet the high level expectations in modern teaching.

5 Students' Feedback

The described method for technological enhanced teaching was developed in the frame of a Grundtvig Learning Partnership starting from 2008 until 2010 and tested in the school year 2009/10. The first feedback was encouraging and the feedback of the students was used as an impact to improve the method and to amend teaching using various hints given by students.

Five years later and enriched by some new experience in teaching, it is time to run another evaluation. For this several questions were expressed and checked in an empirical study. This study follows the common procedure.

5.1 Empirical Research

To evaluate the teaching method, the teaching process and the perception of the students a small empirical study using a normative approach was performed. The intensive normative research aims to improve the use of the described teaching method as a whole and to find potential amendments.

The teaching method is focusing on onsite teaching in which students use multiple devices during class.

5.1.1 Research questions

The core questions of the study for the evaluation of the described teaching method were:

- Do students appreciate the used method and do they see it as an appropriate way for their learning?
- Is the learner-centered approach using multiple devices as the central teaching tool a promising method for the students?

5.1.2 Literature review

The obvious change of the students' preconditions in learning, the learning behaviour and used tools was mentioned first by Prensky (2001) who defined the generation of the digital natives. This new term led to the idea that students can use technology in a natural way and use it as well as a benefit in their learning. There must be a critical analysis of the term "digital natives". The experience of the test phase and the evaluation done in 2016 shows that the so-called digital natives do not exist in the reality or life and all people have to learn a certain level of digital competence.

Smirnova (2008) describes the approach to the use of technical equipment in teaching and describes the necessary steps on faculty level to care for the necessary equipment for using technology in teaching. The focus is on communication and distance learning.

In Europe and other parts of the world, the term "technology-enhanced learning" (TEL) is increasingly used. This new term seems to subsume the term eLearning (which was never defined precisely and used in various and confusing context). Guri-Rosenblit & Gros (2011) state various meanings for the term, often focusing on the delivering of content or the specific support for communication and interaction.

The use of multiple devices as a general tool in learning and teaching and the supplement of the students' technology in onsite teaching by the teaching institution is not mentioned in the currently available studies. The use of Audio-Visual Media, the use of mobile devices or SMART technology[14] is described by Hasan (2014).

The description of the increasing role of the computer in teaching can be found in many teacher-related resources or blogs. What is missing in most of these essays and texts is a pedagogical approach to teach with multiple devices.

Ledesma (2011), for example, describes ideal devices for teaching (like tablets or smart phones using different operating systems), but does not explain how to use them providing a benefit in the students' learning.

---

[14] SMART classroom technology means the collaboration of SMART board and the other devices and workstations that will help to boost the classroom activities.

All the descriptions mentioned before do not characterize the described teaching method at all. The main difference can be found in the different approach of teaching using multiple devices in pure onsite teaching. Therefore, the term "technology enhanced teaching" (or technology enhanced training") with the abbreviation TET (or TETT) is proposed to be used for this special teaching method.

This book describes and explains a new methodology to onsite teaching with a technological enhanced approach based on 5 years of testing and experience. The study is going to approve the tested approach, to produce an insight into the feedback of the students and to provide proposals for amendments.

5.1.3 Idea behind the teaching method

For the so-called digital inhabitants it is common to use various mobile devices always and everywhere. Hence in teaching these common tools should play a more important role and benefit to the outcomes of the students' learning. To care for an adequate added value using multiple devices in teaching a pedagogical framework is necessary. This framework must include a pedagogical concept, a well-fitting instructional design, concepts for managing class and finally an assessment strategy. All these efforts should care for better learning results.

5.1.4 Data description

The used data was collected by a questionnaire and focus groups.

The questionnaire was sent do 76 students using LimeSurvey[15] as a web-based tool. Lime Survey is a tool widely used at universities and other institutions. It allows an anonymous questioning but offers a token-based tracking of the addressed people and their answers. Using reminders, it is possible to collect data from the majority of the addressed people.

---

[15] https://www.limesurvey.org/

Figure 28: The used survey system for the questionnaire (LimeSurvey)

94.7 % of the addressed students, in numbers 72, answered the questions completely after receiving the invitation of the survey followed by 2 reminders; 5 answers were incomplete.

In the data processing, the 4 options in the Likert Scale are replaced by the values 1 – 4 to enable the calculating of an average and the standard deviation.

5.1.5 The questionnaire

The questionnaire provided 17 questions ordered in three groups. The first question group addressed the work with laptops or multiple devices during class. The second group contained questions about teaching materials, like videos and equipment. Finally, the third part asked for typical items during class work, like teamwork of students and the function of the teacher during class.

In the following text, all questions are discussed and interpreted. A special focus is laid to the different approach of male and female students and the resulting different answers. In some cases, the results are overlapping and more or less identically, in several cases an obvious difference can be realized. This should be considered in the future in coeducation, because obviously differences in the learning and the needs of male and female students are visible.

To calculate concrete means and deviations the Likert scale is transferred to numbers:

Likert statement	Used number
I completely agree	1
I partly agree	2
I do not really agree	3
I totally disagree	4

Table 2: *Transfer of the statements of the Likert Scale to numbers*

Using this transformation, "1" represents the best value with highest level of appreciation and "4" the worst value with highest level of disagreement.

5.1.6 The use of a computer makes it easy to contribute class.

This question addressed the students' opinion about their learning and how it can be made easier (with the same success level). Jacob (2009) states his opinion about the use of computers in language learning in a paper, which said that the "use of computer technology makes the class more interesting". Especially the use of multimedia based material is seen as an advantage for the learning of the students and as a motivating component. In the same paper, she names missing pedagogical concepts as a problem.

In the described teaching method, the computer plays an important role combined with a very mature and sophisticated pedagogical framework.

The feedback of the students makes the appreciation of this kind of teaching and their satisfaction visible.

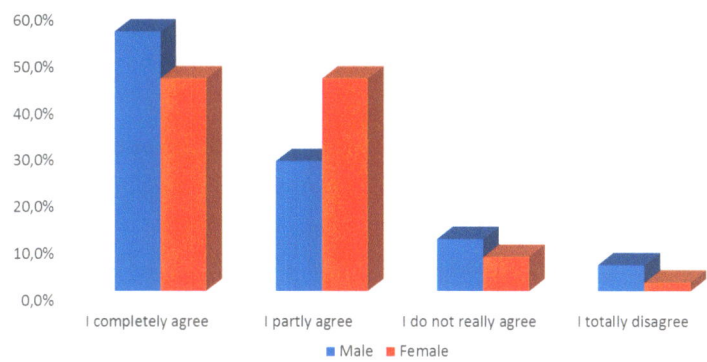

Figure 29: The use of computer as an advantage in learning

	Male	Female
I completely agree	55,6%	45,5%
I partly agree	27,8%	45,5%
I do not really agree	11,1%	7,3%
I totally disagree	5,6%	1,8%
Mean value (total)	1,67	
standard deviation	0,74	

Table 3: Use of the computer as a benefit

The majority of students agrees to the statement. An interesting fact is the shifting of percentage from male to female students. The satisfaction obviously is higher in the male student group. In the same way, more male students deny the benefit.

The result may be seen as a hint to watch female students using the computer during class and to find out, if there exist obstacles or other issues which concerns the group of female students. Stöger (2012) mentions the effect of "gender doing", maybe this is a reason for the difference between male and female students.

5.1.7 The availability of core texts supports the contribution in class.

Taking notes is an appropriate and approved means of learning and contributes to the acquisition of knowledge (Howe, 1974). This fact must be reviewed in modern times in the group of digital natives.

Boch (2005, p. 102) points to the problem of taking notes and that students have to learn in an appropriate way. Especially the way a student takes notes is an individual process and must be learned and practised.

To provide a kind of guidelines to the expected notes, students are supplied with a basic text file which contains the relevant headings of the chapter. In special cases additional text segments are included as well as complicate formulas.

To strengthen the digital competences students are urged to use the necessary tools like the formula editor (integrated in standard word processing programs) for their notes.

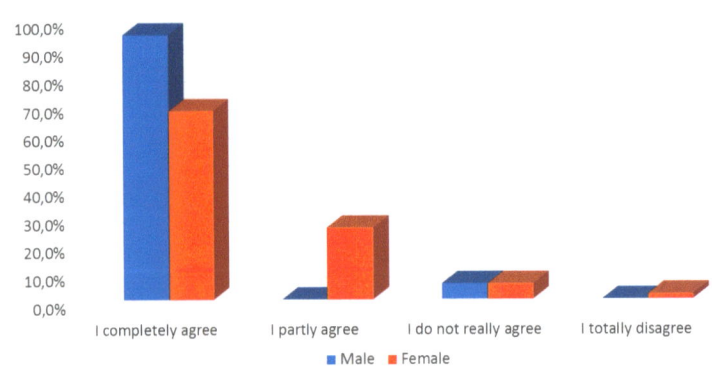

Figure 30: Benefit of the core texts

	Male	Female
I completely agree	94,4%	67,3%
I partly agree	0,0%	25,5%
I do not really agree	5,6%	5,5%
I totally disagree	0,0%	1,8%
Mean value (total)	1,34	
Standard deviation	0,65	

Table 4: *Benefit of the core texts*

The majority of students appreciate the availability of the mentioned texts. The difference between male and female students is not really clear and cannot be explained easily.

5.1.8 PowerPoint® Presentations make contribution in class and taking of notes easier.

The content taught to the students during class is prepared as PowerPoint presentations. These presentations include the used graphics and the formulas in a simple way. These presentations are also available as animates presentations in the eLearning platform.

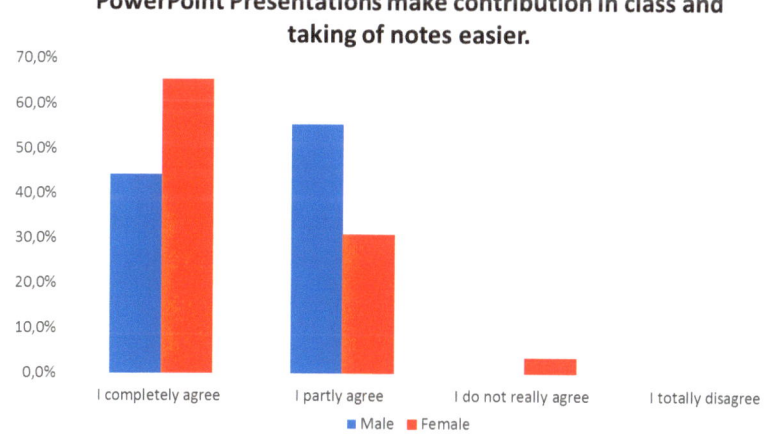

Figure 31: *Benefits of the use of PowerPoint presentations*

	Male	Female
I completely agree	44,4%	65,5%
I partly agree	55,6%	30,9%
I do not really agree	0,0%	3,6%
I totally disagree	0,0%	0,0%
Mean value (total)	1,42	
Standard deviation	0,55	

Table 5: *Benefits of the use of PowerPoint presentations*

Obviously, students appreciate this type of teaching and find the presentations as a useful and promising method. The difference between male and female students cannot be explained easily. A reason can be found in the different approach to follow class.

5.1.9 Standardized graphics, which are used in texts, enable a well taking of notes in an easy way.

Multimedia elements in teaching make it easier for students to understand the context of the taught item or the relation of dependent facts, or other difficult relations. Ayres (2014, p. 206) describes the problem of the split-attention and recommends to use material which do not split the attention of the learner.

Clark & Lyons (2010) mention the advantage of properly designed and created graphic material in teaching. Many interesting hints and guidelines are given in their book.

Therefore, graphics, drawings and images are delivered with the material package of the chapter and inserted in the taken notes based on the core document one by one. So the attention is focused on the content and the relation to the text. Another advantage is the fact that all students use the same multimedia material which is stated as correct and well-fitting to the taught items.

In special cases, simple graphics are created using the features of word. From the pedagogical view, this is an appropriate way to address the attention. Additional, everything done on their own deepens the understanding of the students as well as the indentation of the context.

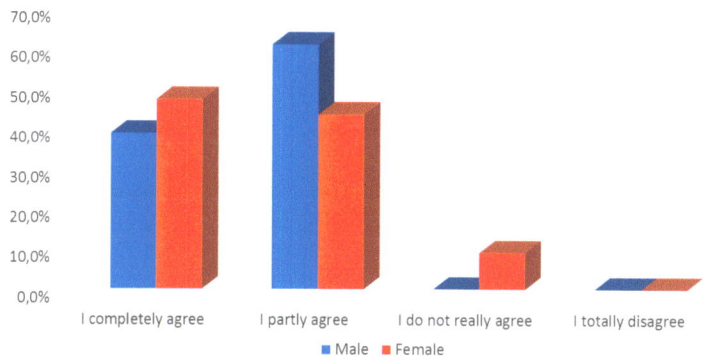

Figure 32: Benefits of the used graphics

The majority of students appreciate the existence of the provided graphics and use it for their notes. Obvious is a difference between male and female students.

	Male	Female
I completely agree	38,9%	47,3%
I partly agree	61,1%	43,6%
I do not really agree	0,0%	9,1%
I totally disagree	0,0%	0,0%
Mean value (total)	1,62	
Standard deviation	0,61	

Table 6: Benefits of the used graphics

The provision of graphical material which is included can be seen as an appropriate way to foster the learning success of the students and it seems to be appreciated. An additional side effect is the increasing practice in using word processing programs by creating well-performed notes including text and graphics.

5.1.10 Multimedia presentations which are uploaded on the online learning platform support studying and reflecting learning matters.

All shown PowerPoint presentations are converted into Shockwave files and uploaded to the eLearning platform as a repository of class presentations. These presentations can be displayed easily with the currently used web browsers (using the Flash® plugin[16]). The material for the various chapters is available as ZIP files at the platform as well.

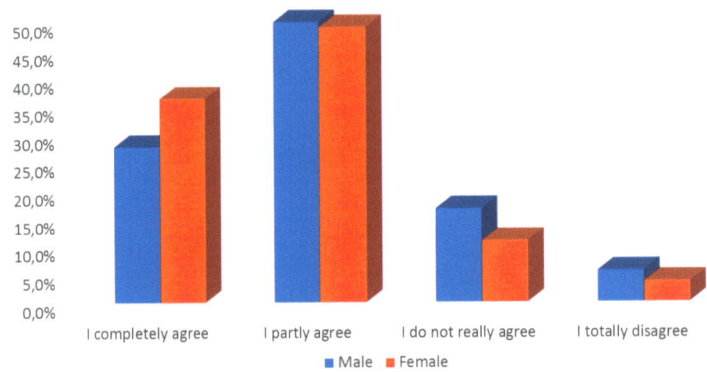

Figure 33: Appreciation of the multimedia based presentations at the learning platform

This is a help for students in a double way:

- Students who missed lessons have the possibility to see exactly the same presentation as their colleagues have seen.

---

[16] Flash is an outdated product and it seems that Adobe will not support a further development of this program, especially being displayed in a web browser. Nevertheless, other technologies will take over in the future.

- Students can watch the presentations at any place at any time as often as they like (or need it). This option employs the features of distance learning with the possibility of independent self-paced learning.

	Male	Female
I completely agree	27,8%	36,4%
I partly agree	50,0%	49,1%
I do not really agree	16,7%	10,9%
I totally disagree	5,6%	3,6%
Mean value (total)	1,86	
standard deviation	0,78	

Table 7: Appreciation of the multimedia based presentations at the learning platform

The results of the survey show a higher level of appreciation of the multimedia based presentations at the learning platform by the female students. Obviously female students use the material for their learning process, to reflect the taught content especially before assessments or tests. Another interpretation is that male students either do not need the material for the reflection, because they have got the essentials from listening to the lessons, or they do not work as carefully as their female colleagues and simply are not interested to watch the presentations again. This interpretation should be further researched under the aspect of different approach of male and female students to science learning.

5.1.11 The use of videos and animations supports the understanding of learning matters.

CITEd [17] (2016) describe in their papers that the use of virtual labs (simulations) and other multimedia material like videos support the learners learning process and progress. For physics, many videos of a high

---

[17] http://www.cited.org/index.aspx?page_id=141

quality and value for the learning are available. Some are in German language, the most of them are in English. As the students must learn English and to finish school at a level of minimum B2, for many of them with C1, English language in videos is not a problem. Videos are used regularly for either presentation during class, as the impact for group work (mostly done by pairs of students), or as additional material provided at the eLearning platform.

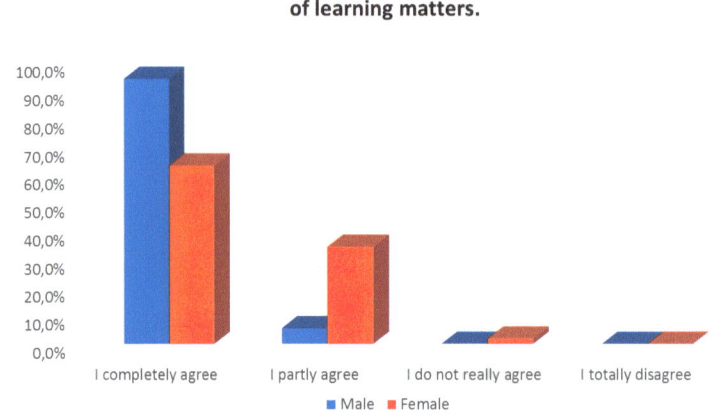

Figure 34: Appreciation of videos and animations to increase the understanding

	Male	**Female**
I completely agree	94,4%	63,6%
I partly agree	5,6%	34,5%
I do not really agree	0,0%	1,8%
I totally disagree	0,0%	0,0%
Mean value (total)	1,30	
Standard deviation	0,49	

Table 8: Appreciation of videos and animations to increase the understanding

Almost all male students agree that videos support the learning matters, but only two thirds of the female students. This is a little bit astonishing and should be researched further. Nevertheless, all students agree more or less that these videos are estimated as useful and helpful for the understanding.

5.1.12 I would like to watch more videos of different learning matters.

Watching videos is an option to show and demonstrate something that is not possible to demonstrate directly in hands-on experiments (due to the fact that the necessary equipment is not available or is broken currently). Videos can open the mind; they can build a base to discussions as well as an impact to deeper understanding. It is astonishing that 20 % of the students (male equal female) are not interested in watching more videos.

I would like to watch more videos of different learning matters.

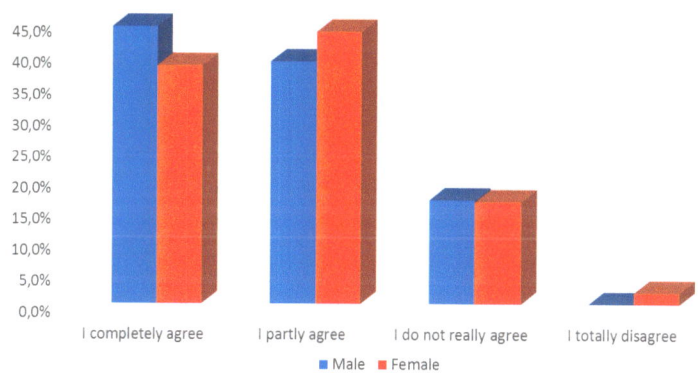

Figure 35: Interest to watch more videos

	Male	Female
I completely agree	44,4%	38,2%
I partly agree	38,9%	43,6%
I do not really agree	16,7%	16,4%
I totally disagree	0,0%	1,8%
Mean value (total)	1,79	
Standard deviation	0,76	

Table 9: Interest to watch more videos: Interest to watch more videos

The mean value is near to 2 with a standard deviation of approximately 0.8 which is significant to a not so high level of agreement. This can be interpreted that the numbers of videos is sufficient (as the students agree to the use and the benefit this does not mean that the students see the use of videos as useless).

5.1.13 Experiments (as long as the necessary materials are available) increase the value of class.

Hands-on experiments are an essential impact to the learning in science and scientific subjects. The best method is probably to let the students work out different tasks on their own. This is not possible due to the non-available material, instruments and technical equipment. An alternative are central undertaken hands-on experiments done by the teacher and assisted by students. Additional the use of virtual labs is an option.

Nevertheless, students want to follow the practical demonstrations and see them as an enrichment for the learning.

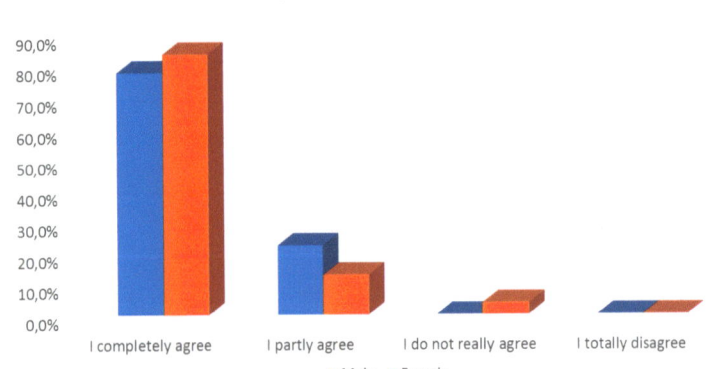

Figure 36: *The evaluation of hands-on experiments*

	Male	Female
I completely agree	77,8%	83,6%
I partly agree	22,2%	12,7%
I do not really agree	0,0%	3,6%
I totally disagree	0,0%	0,0%
Mean value (total)	1,21	
standard deviation	0,47	

Table 10: *The evaluation of hands-on experiments*

Experiments are a special impact and play a central role in teaching physics. In the field of school education, in which general education is a crucial issue the limited time foreseen for class, the pressure to fulfil the curriculum and the missing equipment are obstacles to perform numerous hands-on experiments. The teacher must care for a selection and integrate the students intensively into the running hands-on activity.

Students must take notes, write minutes or summarize what they have seen. Taking pictures by the students for the reason of producing a documentation of what they have seen is another option.

Obviously all students appreciate the hands-on experiments and see it as a valuable contribution to their learning.

The documentation of the experiments is a special issue and, from the point of view of the teacher, often not done properly by the students. Here further steps will be set in the technology enhanced teaching to develop promising strategies and methods of optimized documentation of the seen experiments.

An unsolved problem is that sometimes students miss the experiments and therefore manifest a lack of information, understanding and knowledge. As this experience occurred more often in the past classes a new strategy using the eLearning platform is developed to publish the approved documentation of a student at the platform. This makes available the content and the summary of the experiment to others who have missed something during the performance.

5.1.14 I would like to work with my partner more often together in class, to work out different sections of learning matters.

Active learning is a well-known approach (Bonwell, 1991) and used in modern teaching in various ways. Therefore, partner work was an integrated part of the teaching on several levels.

Biggs (2007, p. 107) also refers to the group work not so much as teaching activities but as teaching situations with a high level of benefit for the learners.

The omnipresent level was the collegial assistance, especially in managing the multiple devices, to clear problems (for examples using the formula editor of the word processor or to manage the also omnipresent network troubles occurring every day).

Another level was the development of solutions, the answering of open questions, and the analyses of upcoming questions during class. The question 9 focused on these items.

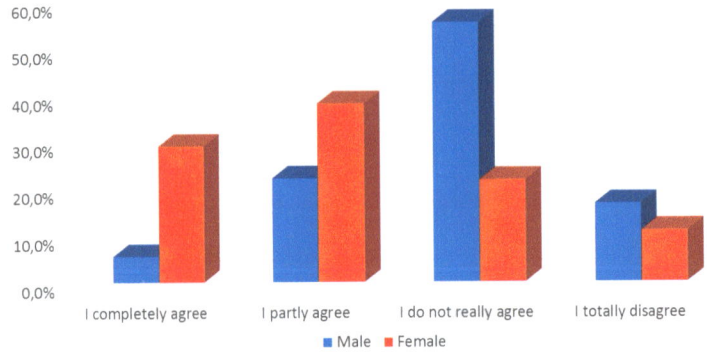

Figure 37: Appreciation of group work of two

	Male	Female	Total
I completely agree	5,6%	29,1%	23,3%
I partly agree	22,2%	38,2%	34,2%
I do not really agree	55,6%	21,8%	30,1%
I totally disagree	16,7%	10,9%	12,3%

Mean value (total)	2,32
Standard deviation	0,96

Table 11: Appreciation of group work of two

The processed data shows a more or less equal distribution of the answers (also visible at the high value of the standard deviation), but the tendency to denying the partner work is visible (see column "Total"). The most interesting result is the discrepancy between male and female students. Male students obviously do not appreciate these kinds of group work. Female students are more indifferent.

In the focus groups this issue was inquired to the students. The given feedback indicates to a higher social competence of the female students, especially in non-mixed teams, female students appreciate working together. Younger students with an age of 10 to 11 years like to undertake work in pairs (for example in informatics lessons). The results seem to depend on the age, the taught subject, and on the specific group constellation. These facts should be part of a further research work.

5.1.15 The teacher, who teaches in class, should communicate the learning matters to students.

This question asked for the role and the expected engagement of the teacher. The role of a teacher in active learning could be more equal to a moderator who cares for the students and assist them in their learning process (This is natural in Active Distance Learning). In the situation of a teacher being live in the classroom students expect active input from the teacher. The teacher guides the class, presents questions, content, involves the students actively in the learning process, but must be available to explain the content, difficult context and supply the students with the necessary knowledge of the subject.

The students expect the teacher to be the expert, a scientific authority with huge consolidated knowledge, expertise, and background knowledge. This coincides to the results of the Hattie study and Hattie's book (2014), which describes teachers as a source of ideas and knowledge.

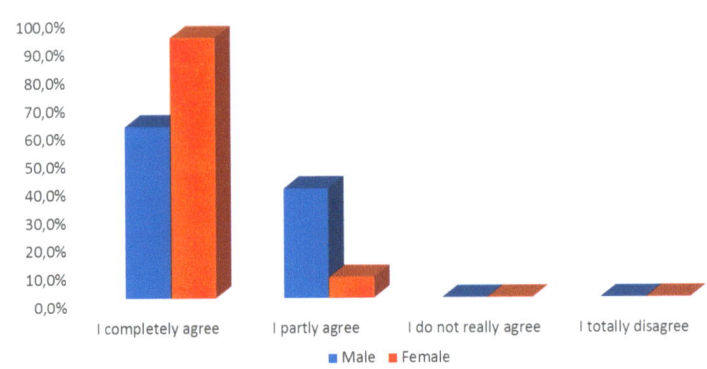

Figure 38: *The role of the teacher*

	Male	Female	Total
I completely agree	61,1%	92,7%	84,9%
I partly agree	38,9%	7,3%	15,1%
I do not really agree	0,0%	0,0%	0,0%
I totally disagree	0,0%	0,0%	0,0%
Mean value (total)	1,15		
Standard deviation	0,36		

Table 12: *The role of the teacher*

While the majority of the students agree to the role of a teacher as to be responsible for the learning matters an interesting difference occurs between male and female students. Less than two thirds of the male students see the teacher's work focussing on the core teaching process. The female students obviously have a different approach to the role of the teacher.

This must be seen in context with the next question.

5.1.16 During class the teacher should encourage students to take actively part in class, for example with the aid of questions and discussions.

Active teaching forces students to play a certain part in the teaching process. In the discussed method, students are involved during lectures and presentation to answer open questions, to perform critical thinking, and to analyse class-related situations. This can be done in individual addressing single students as well as a group work of two or in bigger groups.

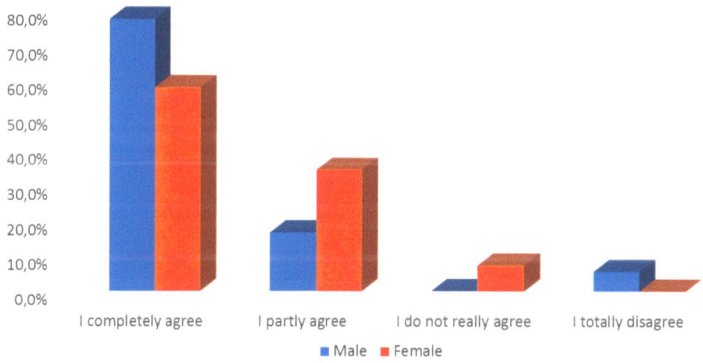

Figure 39: Appreciation of being actively involved into the teaching process

Here the results of the processed data are different. Female students do not agree in that level as the male students.

This can be interpreted as the male students prefer to think about specific questions while the female students like to get explained the context and do not like to be addressed during lessons.

	Male	Female	Total
I completely agree	77,8%	58,2%	63,0%
I partly agree	16,7%	34,5%	30,1%
I do not really agree	0,0%	7,3%	5,5%
I totally disagree	5,6%	0,0%	1,4%

Mean value (total)	1,45
Standard deviation	0,66

Table 13: *Appreciation of being actively involved into the teaching process*

Nevertheless, both groups of students basically approach to be involved actively in the teaching. The small group of students who are not really interested to be active are a small minority.

5.1.17 The online learning platform provides students with additional multimedia presentations and the presentations which are shown in class. I watch these regularly.

The online learning platform based on a Moodle server provides all the material presented or used in class. The intention is to offer the students a repository in which they can access the original material, the seen presentations or the used graphics, animations or videos.

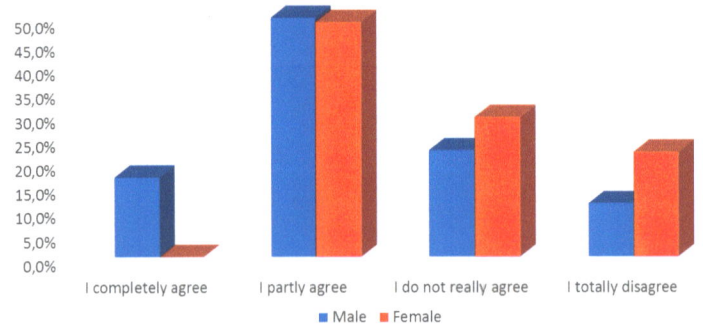

Figure 40: *Use of the eLearning platform*

The eLearning server also has the function to provide the material to students who have missed a lesson, so that they can catch up what they have missed.

	Male	Female
I completely agree	16,7%	0,0%
I partly agree	50,0%	49,1%
I do not really agree	22,2%	29,1%
I totally disagree	11,1%	21,8%
Mean value (total)	2,62	
Standard deviation	0,84	

Table 14: Use of the eLearning platform

The students give the feedback that they do not use the platform intensively. The average of 2.62 with a standard deviation of 0.8 shows a low percentage of accessing the repositories.

An interesting fact is that more male students make use of the available material. In the focus round, they confess that accessing the platform is done before assessments because they are not sure about their own completed notes.

Due to this fact, the repository plays a role in the learning and students behavior. Taking notes is not controlled in a strict way because students of the age up from 16 should be able and be sensible enough to take notes in a serious and stringent way. Nevertheless, this seems to be an optimistic approach. Male students are used to compensate missing facts or content from their notes by using the learning platform.

5.1.18 Working with laptop in class has improved my computer skills.

The tendency to presume ICT knowledge to digital inhabitants is a typical sign of our times. In reality, this is only partly true. Even if the students grow up in a world full of computers and technics it is not natural that they have profound knowledge of the use of computers or the related software. It is clear that the students have to gain the competences of appropriate use of their multiple devices as well as the necessary knowledge. This has been done in former classes so the students have a high level of competence in ICT. This may be the reason why the answers are so equal distributed – some learned something new and others not.

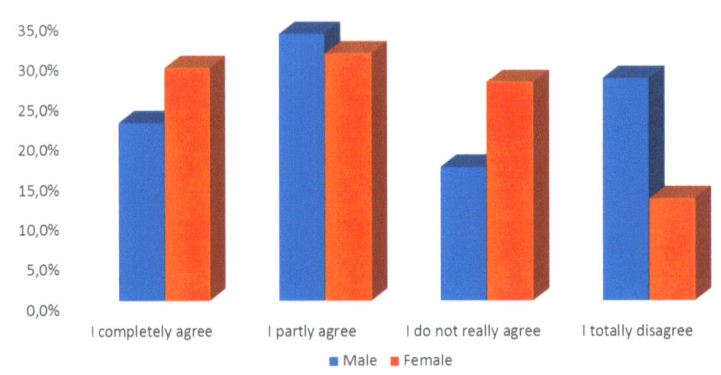

Figure 41: Improvement of computer skills

	Male	Female
I completely agree	22,2%	29,1%
I partly agree	33,3%	30,9%
I do not really agree	16,7%	27,3%
I totally disagree	27,8%	12,7%
Mean value (total)	2,30	
Standard deviation	1,04	

Table 15: Improvement of computer skills

The technology enhanced teaching requires basic competences in the use of the hardware, operating system and the related software. Especially in teaching science, the use of a formula editor or the creating of simple graphics is necessary and must be handled quickly and stringent by the students.

It is a tragically misbelief that it could be possible to gain the necessary competences in ICT during the learning of a specific subject. In such settings, neither the competence in the subject nor the necessary digital literacy can be created in a satisfying way. It is simply necessary to care for the needed competences in ICT before the use of technology or multiple devices in teaching.

5.1.19 Working with laptop in class has improved my skills in different programs (as word).

Technical enhanced teaching needs preliminary competences in ICT. Nevertheless, the practical use of the multiple devices increases the competences in using software in a practical way, for example to take notes, to insert simple self-made graphics using the graphical features of the word processing program, or the formula editor integrated in the word processing tools.

Working to develop the necessary computer literacy, for example in typical assignments far from reality, is completely different to the practical use. In this situation of technical enhanced learning, students have to proof their competence, knowledge and skills. Lessons claim a permanent increasing of ICT literacy which leads to a high level of competences to use multiple devices.

Most students in class are equipped with a laptop using Windows® as the operating system and are working with Microsoft Word® as the word processing program. This environment provides more or less a homogenous setting and it is possible to explain special issues in taking notes (like foreign characters or special formula problems) during the lesson[18].

In the first year of technology enhanced teaching all necessary skills must be developed by the students as quickly as possible, otherwise the students are distracted from the learning and understanding the taught physical content by solving their computer problems.

---

[18] The precondition is an extremely high level in computer literacy of the teacher.

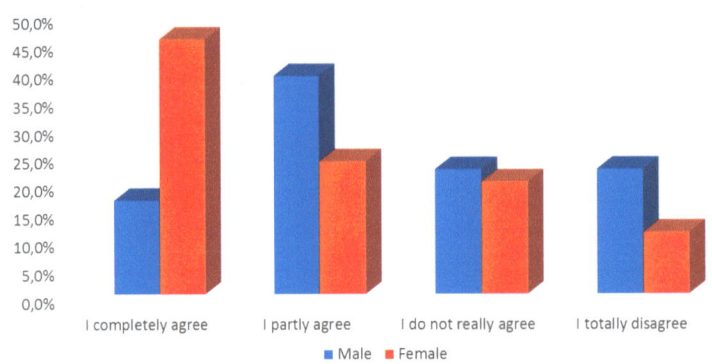

Figure 42: Improve of skills in using specific computer programs

	Male	Female
I completely agree	16,7%	45,5%
I partly agree	38,9%	23,6%
I do not really agree	22,2%	20,0%
I totally disagree	22,2%	10,9%
Mean value (total)	2,10	
Standard deviation	1,06	

Table 16: Improve of skills in using specific computer programs

The feedback of the students shows that female students benefit more from that kind of teaching. The high level of strict agreement can be interpreted that the female students had the chance to increase their computer literacy more than the male students. More than 60 % of all students confessed that they could benefit through the lessons in the field of ICT.

For the teacher, this is a very interesting result because currently the opinion dominates that young people from the generation of the digital natives have the necessary computer competence and also the ICT literacy to use standard programs like word processing tools on a high standard. The results of the study prove that even in classes well educated in ICT literacy the level can be increased by simply measures like taking notes using the standard features of the programs.

5.1.20 The ability to type without looking on the laptop is essential for these type of classes.

Students use typewriting to take notes during class. The average writing speed of a student is around 0.3 to 0.4 words/second, whereas a lecturer speaks at a rate of around 2 to 3 words/second (Boch, 2005, p. 102). To follow the presentations and to take notes efficiently it is necessary to learn typewriting on a professional way. The students, who were asked for the survey in this book, should have learned to write approximately 100 characters per minute, which means 12 – 14 words per minute. This should be sufficient for producing well-done notes covering the presented contend and to summarize the gained knowledge.

A problem is that many students do not practice the typewriting or never have learned it in the foreseen speed.

Another problem is the missing competence to take notes containing all the information which is necessary to learn, to reflect and to memorise the gained knowledge (as part of the learner competences). Boch (2005, p. 106) mentions this problem and offers appropriate and practicable solutions.

From the point of view of the teacher not all students were at the level, in which they could take notes in the necessary foreseen speed. Here is the students' view to this topic: The mean value indicates that the students do not believe that typewriting is a crucial issue. They estimate that it is possible to take notes in an appropriate way without these specific skills. Nevertheless, they all learned blind typewriting with ten fingers and therefore are more experienced as the average of the digital natives who did not learn it or practice it.

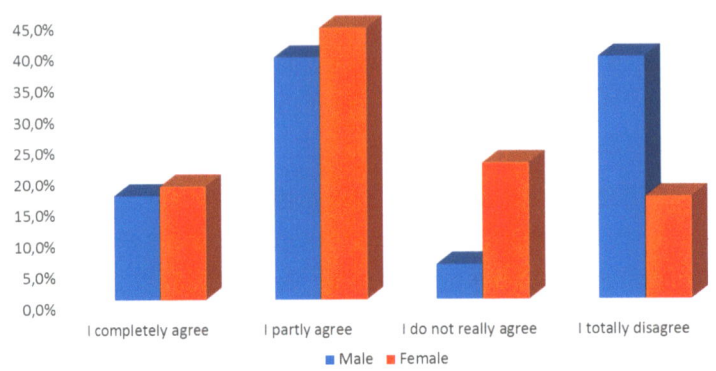

Figure 43: Know typewriting to take notes - students' view

	Male	Female
I completely agree	16,7%	18,2%
I partly agree	38,9%	43,6%
I do not really agree	5,6%	21,8%
I totally disagree	38,9%	16,4%
Mean value (total)	2,67	
Standard deviation	1,15	

Table 17: Students need to know typewriting

Male students do not see the necessity to learn typewriting as an issue, they deny the need of these skills at a high level. In this special case further activities must be planned to find out the level of the quality of the taken notes.

The high value of the standard deviation is an indicator for a wide spread of different opinions among the students, which are well visible in the chart.

5.1.21 I would use provided videos for learning matters for studying at home (as preparation or for working out learning matters on my own at home).

Videos as a typical multimedia based material are a mighty tool to either understand difficult physical processes or to reflect what students have learned during class.

Videos provided at the eLearning platform or linked from YouTube to the eLearning platform are foreseen in technology enhanced learning as additional material for the students. There exist many offers of CC[19]-licensed learning videos.

Altherr et alt (2003) mention that it is easy to find multimedia material for teaching physics, but at a closer look the free available material does not provide the excellent quality that is needed.

Nevertheless, some material exists and can be used for the students to supply their learning. The students use this material in a restricted way and not so often. The feedback of the students does not show significant differences between male and female students.

Basically, the students would use additional video material.

The precondition for additional videos are:

- Videos must fit to the chapter,
- should have a high level of quality,
- should be in an acceptable length, and
- should be a good complementary approach to the competences taught in class.

These preconditions were found out analysing the focus groups' feedback.

---

[19] Creative Commons, https://creativecommons.org/

I would use provided videos for learning matters for studying at home (as preparation or for working out learning matters on my own at home).

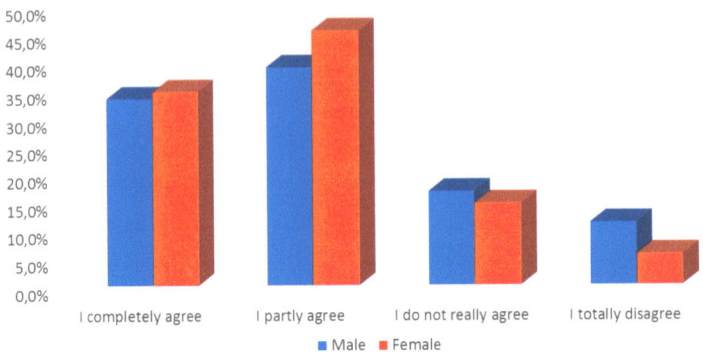

Figure 44: Students would use videos for learning at home

	Male	Female
I completely agree	33,3%	34,5%
I partly agree	38,9%	45,5%
I do not really agree	16,7%	14,5%
I totally disagree	11,1%	5,5%
Mean value (total)	1,95	
Standard deviation	0,87	

Table 18: Students would use videos for learning at home

The willingness of the students is more or less existing to watch additional videos at home in their free time. The standard deviation shows a broader variance distributed around the partly agreement. This is a typical effect of different learning cultures of the students; some would like to have more multimedia material while others are satisfied with the videos they have seen during class and others prefer to reflect the content using their notes.

5.1.22 How long should videos for studying at home or preparing or working out learning matters last in your opinion?

Various videos were used in the past years and students watched them in class or also at home. Weatherhead (2014) published an article in "The Guardian" with the statement, that young people, due to the rapid adoption of smart phones and tablet computers in context with streaming technology and permanent Internet connection, are used to consume multimedia content everywhere and at any time. An interesting fact is the attention time: Dowell (2015) estimates this value with 2 to three minutes. Steinberg (2012) found out that young consumers from the digital natives' generation switch media 27 times the hour, which means a continuous watching of the content for 2 minutes in average. Even if that case study only covers a sample of 30 it indicates that digital natives prefer to watch short videos or, in other words, videos must be short to attract the students. This background was the intention for the question about an acceptable length of videos for studying.

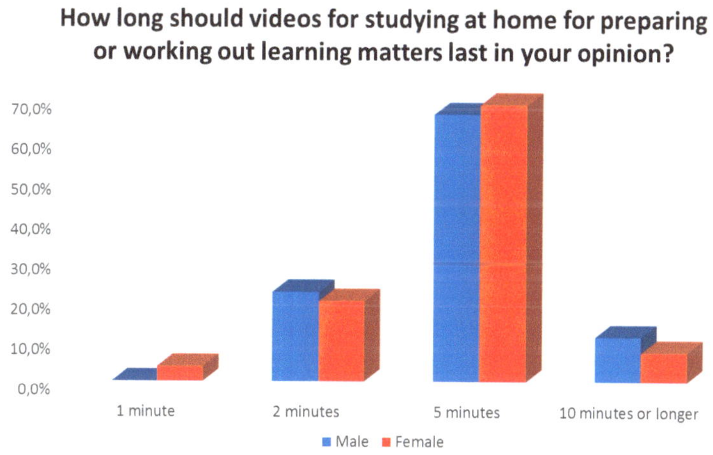

Figure 45: How long can videos last to be watched by students

	Male	Female
1 minute	0,0%	3,6%
2 minutes	22,2%	20,0%
5 minutes	66,7%	69,1%
10 minutes or longer	11,1%	7,3%
Mean value (total)	2,82	
Standard deviation	0,60	

Table 19: How long can videos last to be watched by students

The study proves more or less the meaning of the experts. For the purpose of learning videos, the length of five minutes is accepted from the majority. Well-produced videos with a duration of five minutes are difficult to organize. Teachers have to take out the relevant parts from longer videos and to re-edit videos. For the Austrian schools no problem of copyright violation is evident if the videos are only used in a non-public learning environment (of a public school).

5.2   Open Questions

The open questions focused on two items:

- Which issues of the learning experience using technology enhanced teaching did satisfy you?
- Which obstacles and problems did you realize and do you have any idea how these problems could be fixed or changes?

The open questions were answered by approximately 40 students, less than 20 mentioned problems, obstacles and issues that should be changed.

5.2.1   Satisfying issues of the learning experience

Exactly 35 students gave feedback about positive issues in their learning experience. The majority dealt with taking notes and the use of the multiple device as a tool during class.

Taking notes

The most named items were in relation to taking notes. So the students see an advantage in the use of a laptop or notebook (as the most used multiple device). As a benefit the students mention that

- it is easier to take notes with the laptop than by pencil and paper,
- the organisation of notes is more stringent using a simple organisation structure of the files collecting them in a folder,
- it is easy to insert graphics into the document and also to exchange them (if necessary),
- the speed of taking notes is higher at the laptop than in handwriting,
- it is easy to complete missing parts (due to missed lessons) and to catch up missed lessons,
- taking notes with the laptop makes it more simple to follow the presentations,
- it is possible to exchange documents easily by email,
- the notes are in a better form and more legibly than handwriting,
- the available basic structure makes it easy keep an order in the documents,
- the prepared document enables students to concentrate more on the lecture, the discussions, and the additional presented and discussed content,
- the laptop makes the reflection of the notes easier.

The feedback referring to the notes taking reflects that the method offers a big benefit, especially in following class, to the students.

Culture of studying and learning technology

Another mentioned issue focuses on the studying technique. The students appreciate the well-organized material which was created during class. From the point of view of the teacher it seems to be obvious that this feedback was given by well-organized students who know how to organize the folders, where to save texts and other related material. This finding confirms the need to instruct students in an early stage how to manage and to organise their notes and material.

Students mentioned the permanently necessary involvement during class to create satisfying notes and complete documents, which are necessary for successful reflections and assessments.

The method uncovers the need to develop an individual learning style because each student is used to learn in an individual and personal style. This makes it almost unable to exchange the taken notes for successful reflections.

Several students mentioned also the method as a convenient and successful method to follow class. Students always know exactly what currently is on schedule and which content or competence is to be processed now.

Advantage of the PowerPoint presentations

The PowerPoint presentations enable a pleasantly and efficiently taking of notes. The slides offer a great and easy to understand overview of the taught content or competence and can be easily enhanced and completed by the students in their individual way to take notes.

Use of the learning platform

Students see an advantage of the learning platform as a repository of relevant sources during class. Additional the offer of complementary documents to the followed lessons is appreciated.

The students pointed out a typical advantage of eLearning: the "anytime and anywhere availability of the content of the learning platform"

Other statements

The use of multiple devices makes it easy to check content or items quickly in the Internet. Furthermore, the lessons force students to practice and improve their computer literacy permanently during class.

5.2.2 Obstacles, problems and amendment proposals

The permanent use of multiple devices includes the risk of distraction. The students mention that they were induced to do other things during class simply misled from the fact that it is possible. For example, checking some fact in the Internet let student visit their Facebook account afterwards or to check their emails (Most students use a web-based email provider).

Another mentioned item was the problem to take notes. Here students complain about lacking practice in note taking or the missing pace in typewriting. So, they are too slow to follow class and the presentations. This leads to incomplete notes and makes it difficult to reflect the content.

Proposed amendments

Several students recommend a more intensive and active involvement into the learning process. This could be done by more hands-on experiments performed by students' groups as well as by more frequently done case studies or examples that must be discussed by the students.

One student meant that too much text in the prepared document decreases the need to take notes personally and that the process of taking notes by writing increases the learning success. This student recommends to keep the basic texts provided for the students short.

Another student complained about the small number or audio-visual material and would preferred to get a more intensive visualisation of the content by animations, images and videos.

5.3 Summary

One finding of the study is the different feedback to several questions done by male and female students. Gross (2014) mentions in her posting that teachers have to "understand the different learning styles of boys and girls so that they are able to create a learning environment that meets the needs of both". She mentions a difference between the learning of girls and their counterparts, the boys. The study about technology enhanced teaching proves a different approach to learning, the use of the learning environment and the individual learning. In many cases male and female students behave the same, in other issues there are significant differences visible.

Besides the necessary specific approach, the most students more or less behave similarly and have similar needs. So the most students appreciate the used teaching method and see benefits for their learning being involved in the presented technology enhanced teaching.

They accept the technical approach as a help for taking notes, to use multimedia based content, to organize their work, and to reflect the taught content.

Students would prefer more hands-on experiments, especially with their personal involvement. They would like to be supplied with more multimedia based material and interactive material.

In general, the study proves that the teaching method is well accepted by the students and seen as an appropriate way to gain competences in physics.

6 Lessons Learned

Teaching includes success stories as well as failures. Regarding quality in teaching an appropriate quality enhance framework provides the necessary quality in the teaching process. Quality enhancement can be undertaken in different manners. In the described teaching method, quality enhancement is done by regularly feedback and the use of these results in an amendment process.

Lessons Learned is experience based knowledge or understanding that has a significant impact for a process or an organisation. Positive as well negative issues mix the experience and lead to a complex image of the analysed activity or process. In many cases, it is difficult to find out the positive aspects, to correct the negative impact or to eliminate obstacles.

To balance what has been working successfully and to compare it with what has gone bad is a promising approach for quality enhancement using Lessons Learned.

This chapter reflects the experience taken in the last five years. It is combined with several ideas for amendment and a certain evaluation of the success of the method. An impact to Lessons Learned was given by the students in private discussions or organized focus rounds. Here approximately 120 Students were involved and could give feedback and make amendment proposals. In the review, new insight or new findings from research are included also to offer a kind of quality enhancement of the described method.

6.1 Pros – Cons Balance

For teaching physics, the described method cares for an efficient teaching. The method makes it easy for the students to follow class; it makes the learning more or less effortless for the students. As the method is adapted from lectures, it is a straightforward way to teach students the foreseen knowledge quickly. The method also makes it easy to pass quantity of information to the students. The teacher has the control over what is being taught in the classroom as the responsible person for the source of information.

The method was developed for an onsite teaching environment supplied with an eLearning platform with permanent availability (using the Internet). For motivated students, it is easy to follow the presentations and to gain the foreseen competences. This requires the competence of listening and processing what they have heard combined with the visual impression conveyed by the presentation. To address other types of learner multimedia based content is used and complemented by various hands-on experiments. The method is extremely time efficient, the teacher is the guide to the competences which have to be gained and is open for any questions during class. In relevance to the short time of a maximum of 210 lessons within three years of learning, each lesson lasting 50 minutes (to get a complete outline of physics) the method creates promising results.

As the method is deviated from lectures, it is necessary to use methods of active teaching to involve students in some way, otherwise the method slips to a simple one-way instruction.

Another disadvantage of the method is the lack of self-engagement and the short-kept possibility of active learning. Active learning requests a high level of motivation, interest of the students (which is not yet a strong sense found with the students) and available time. Students, who are strong in other learning styles than auditory learning, have the advantage of following the presentations, but be more challenged to learn and to gain the expected competences.

Students who are weak in note-taking skills will have trouble in selecting the core content, what they should take for their notes and what is important to remember from class. The teacher may not get a real feeling about the gained competences of the students or how much students understand what has been taught.

From the experience of the last five years, the time factor is the biggest obstacle to use various methods of active teaching. Time consuming lab work, which would lead the students to a very high level of understanding can only be done with more available time and with a better (or appropriate designed and compiled) equipment. So these teaching approaches are dedicated to schools with a higher level of competences and enhanced curriculum, in which students can deepen their knowledge and understanding and practice in on-hands experiments what they have learned. These schools provide minimum 280 lessons during the upper high school level.

The issues discussed above lead to a short table with the key items listed in a pros/cons analyses.

PROS	CONS
- Efficient teaching possible (deviated from lectures) - Straightforward teaching conveys knowledge to students quickly - Includes active teaching methods - Multimedia based teaching - Offering hands-on experiments - Efficiently guide students by generalized documents - High level of self-responsibility for the learning of the students	- Only some active teaching methods used - No permanent active involvement of students - Effortless learning does not foster personal engagement - Sometimes one-way instruction - Sometimes teachers do not get the real feeling for how much the students understand - Students who are weak in notes-taking will have troubles to know what is important to remember for good grades - Students may find longer parts of presentations as boring and lose interest in the subject

Table 20: Pros/Cons analyses of key items

6.2 Multimedia and Interactive Materials

The described teaching approach is deviated from lectures added by several items to avoid typical problems of lecture-based teaching. To provide an appropriate change in methods multimedia based sequences are included and interactive material is used.

A serious problem is the lack of appropriate material. For an average teacher, it is not possible to create multimedia based or interactive applications at high level which would be necessary for high school teaching. Simulations free to use are really hard to find and often cannot be used in class due to technical reasons. It is outdated material often, or special software products are needed to run the simulation. Also, many other obstacles can appear. To find well-fitting videos is easier in some way. From various famous universities faculty material exists which can be used for class. The videos are often too long and must be shortened, which is problematic from the point of view of copyright violation. Not all material is licensed under a creative commons license. Special learn videos are provided by various organisations assisting students in their learning and professional companies. As the school does not care for the financial resources only free available material can be taken in account for teaching in class. The most videos for students to learn are offered by companies selling them in the field of business (management training, computer training and similar topics). For the subject physics the offers are poor. Profound knowledge of the English language makes it possible to access also videos produced in English speaking countries.

6.2.1 Videos used in class

The used videos were mostly taken from YouTube [20] using the search feature. Videos were locally downloaded to have them available in any case, for example when the Internet connection in school is broken. The videos are linked to a web-based eLearning server so the students can review them at home as many times as they like. In the eLearning course additional videos (not seen or discussed during class) were offered to provide additional material, especially for the reflection of lectures and presentations at home, or for students who have missed single lessons to have better chances to gain the requested competences.

---

[20] YouTube: https://www.youtube.com/

6.2.2 Interactive material and simulations

Interactive material is only available from professional sellers, from universities or interested people teaching physics. The most material is available as Flash® product, in the most cases as ShockWave[21] file .swf. This format can be easily displayed in web browsers with the installed plugin. Due to the policy of Adobe it can be expected that Flash and the related files are not supported in the future. It is not clear which material will be available, how it is programmed and published within the next years. Also the availability of ShockWave plugins for browsers is not cleared.

To provide students with a simple method all Flash files are converted to stand alone applications using the Flash projector. These programs can be downloaded from the eLearning platform as well as they can be used directly on Windows compatible multiple devices.

6.3 Group Work and Discussions

Group work and discussions are methods to interrupt the presentation and to involve students interactively. Groups are kept small and the work to be done is distributed to pairs of students or groups of three (Laughlin et alt., 2006, p. 694). The reason is to keep the interruption short and organisational background small so the loss of time for the organisation is kept to a low level. Discussions are directly performed in class without changing places.

6.3.1 Simple group work

Group work always starts with a "teaser": a problem dealing with a physical item which increased during a presentation or a short video sequence which is displayed to the students.

The students have to solve the problem in small groups and to create a documentation of their findings. Selected groups present their findings,

---

[21] Shockwave files are seen problematic in web use due to their vulnerability. Locally used shockwave files are not dangerous and will still be used in the next years. There exists the possibility to convert these files in stand-alone application by a viewer.

discuss them with the others classmates, find correct solutions or statements, and take notes of the correct findings.

This type of group work fosters the creativity of solving problems, also critical thinking (by analysing the presentations of other groups considering logical structure or errors) and the competence to express the group findings or outcomes.

An interesting additional aspect is to gain the ability to realize the precise work description of the group work. Students of that age often do not provide the skill to spot exactly what is to be done in the group work and which results or outcomes are expected. This is part of the learning process during the three school years and finally should lead to the competence to realise a precise work description and to solve the named problems in the expected way.

6.3.2 Discussions

Discussions are big group activities and cover the complete class. The number of students is approximately 20 in all classes and offers the possibility to handle the class as one discussion group. Discussions always depend on the participating people. Some students tend to be very inactive during discussions and must be addressed personally by the teacher. The observation of the last five years suggest that it is not always possible to involve all students equally and that this effect is based upon the individual personality (which is highly developed at the age of the involved students). The discussion's result is summarized and must be taken to the notes by the students. The discussions should lead students to analyse problems, to listen to proposals of others, to evaluate them critically and to put them into context of the currently taught topics.

An emphasis during discussions is the context to everyday life and how physics is visible in our daily environment or influences it.

6.3.3 General approach to group work and discussions

Group work and discussions always have a starting activity and a contribution to the notes of the students as a defined end of the activity. They last for some minutes (discussion) or maximum 15 minutes (group work). The duration is mainly depending on the topic, the extent of the taught content and the intensity of involvement of the students.

A typical flow of a discussion is shown in the following figure.

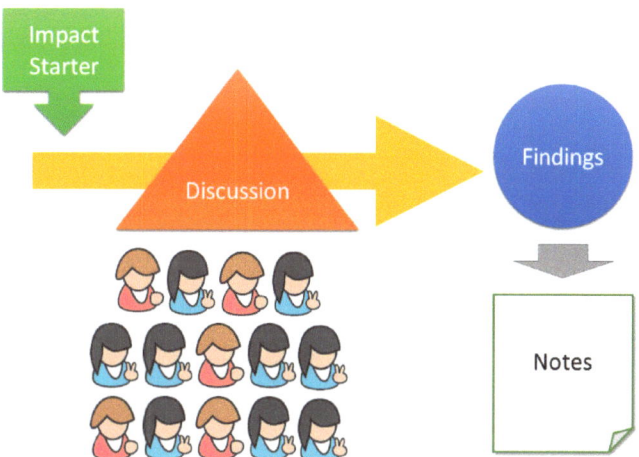

Figure 46: *Flow of a typical discussion*

For students, these activities are always a welcomed interruption of straightforward teaching. Obviously, the maturity of the learners is an important fact (Mazohl 2015). The personal stage of development of a student decides if the student benefits from the discussion or not. Active teaching should address learners, but in the same way, the learners must contribute to the activities and be interested to have a profit of participating in that activity. In group discussions, students often act passively, only some of them follow the discussion without further engagement. For the learning success, this will bring the same as the simple lecture of the teacher. Students always can determine for themselves if they want to learn by being involved actively (This is a basic problem of the motivation of the learner).

6.4 Distance Learning

Distance learning is not a core issue of the teaching but partly plays a certain role in the learning process. The functions of the eLearning platform are:

- Repository of the provided materials (For example the core text files and the graphic packages for the notes)
- Download of interactive or multimedia material
- Additional material for students (for example for reflection)
- Interactive group work (For example forum)
- Upload for assignments (for example material produced during group work)
- Formative assessment (using competence checks created with the test features of Moodle)

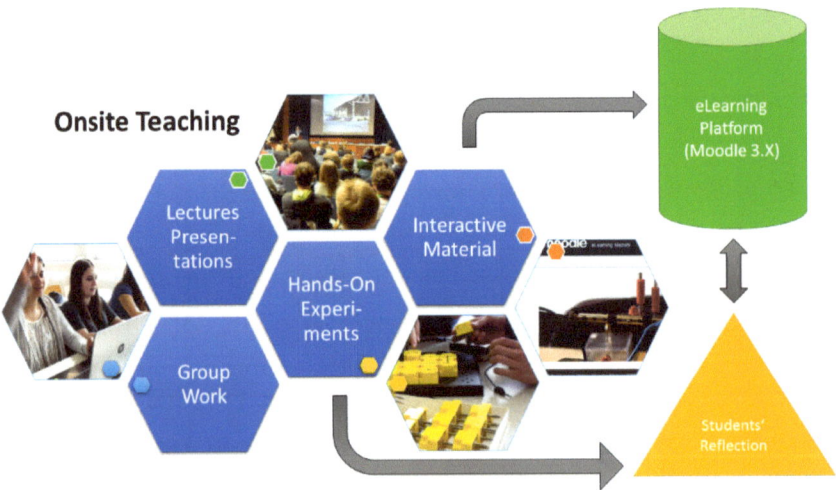

Figure 47: Connection between the work at school, at home and the use of the eLearning platform

The use of the eLearning platform enables an easy distribution of material and the typical distance learning advantages like access to the platform from everywhere at any time. Nevertheless, the described teaching method is no distance learning but a strict and stringent onsite teaching using modern tools and typical resources of so-called digital inhabitants.

The platform supports mobile devices like smart phones as well as typical laptops. It is using a responsive design for the Moodle 3.X and is hosted by an external provider.

6.5 Pedagogical considerations

The described teaching method uses no single didactic or pedagogical approach but a mixture of various methods which were identified as useful and promising for the learning of the students. Therefor several items of the pedagogical approach are used during teaching and provide a mixture of "the best from pedagogical experience and knowledge".

The use of a package of methods offers not only variety for the students but enables the best approach to explain or describe content which is difficult to understand as well. Also the different approach to physics for male and female students should be an issue in teaching. Gross (2014) mentions in her article subtle differences between male and female students and points out that this knowledge helps the teacher to "guide the students in a positive way and to meet better their needs".

6.5.1 Didactics

Teachers using the described method must act in different roles more intensive as in traditional teaching. Besides the motivating and coaching of students the technical aspect gains more and more importance. The teacher must be well prepared to assist the students in their taking notes, plan the use of multimedia and to foresee possible problems and be well prepared for solving them. The education of students to use the multimedia or interactive applications is another issue.

6.5.2 Instructional design

In this technology enhanced teaching method, no single instructional model can be applied to the teaching, it is more or less a mixture of the models explained at the beginning of the book. The successful and promising items taken from the various models are:

- A profound analyses of the competences
  to be learned taking in account the learner characteristics.
- Definition of the learning objectives
  (in near context with the given curriculum and a special focus to the given conditions of the final exams)
- The development of the instructional (or learning) material
  including the creation of chapters containing the basic material for the students. This also covers additional material provided at the eLearning platform or preparation (or compiling) of multimedia material for the class.
- Planning and executing a continuous assessment
  (Carlson, 2003) leading to marks of the students (for their school reports) using a summative evaluation.
- A continuous formative evaluation of the instructional material
  is performed regularly to improve the used material in class.

6.5.3 Learner-centered access

The learner-centered approach in class worked quite well. From the experience of missing skills, the students' time must be reserved to learn to explain, to perform and practice thinking, to analyse arguments, to build correct context and connections, and to evaluate evidence.

All these skills cannot be taught in a short period (with two lessons the week), it takes months and must be practiced over and over again.

The learner-centered approach to teaching should be a school overlapping concept and practiced in all (relevant) subject. This optimistic demand is far from reality and it costs a lot of time to convey the learner-centered skills to the students if it is performed only in one single subject.

Another item, counterproductive to a learner-centered access, is the missing basic knowledge and the missing interest in basic education. In the focus group, an interesting answer was given by a female student: "We don't have to know everything because we can look up everything by Internet". This approach to knowledge, as one of the three columns of competences, makes it almost impossible for certain students to contribute actively to class. For these students, pure strict ex-cathedra teaching with regularly and stringent undertaken assignments seems to be the only way for an acceptable achievement of the foreseen learning goals.

Figure 48: The optimized learner in modern teaching (Source Mazohl)

From the teacher's point of view, the students' maturity, the insight in learning strategies and existing goals are the base for success in teaching with learner-centered setting. Barer-Stein (1993) mentions problems of missing maturity of learners and presents some findings that the maturity of female students of the observed age is better than compared with male students, but this effect was not significantly visible during the study.

6.5.4 Competence based learning outcomes

Competence based teaching is a must in the European Community and part of the description of the curriculum since several years. The teaching and particularly the assignments as well as the assessments are kept using competence descriptions and the various typical keywords for the various competence levels. These are "name a list of …", "explain the …", or "bring into context …". It does not seem to be easy for students to follow the intention of specific questions using these keywords.

The three fields used for the competence based teaching are reproduction (=knowledge), transfer, reflection and problem solving skills.

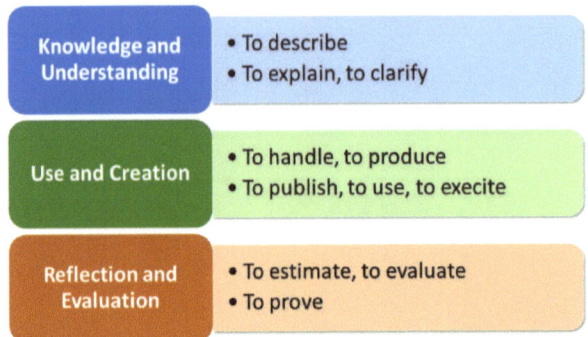

Figure 49: *Key words in context with competence based teaching*

It is obvious that students have to learn and practice competence based questions and answers. Often language problems (not only visible by students with migration background as well as not evident by native speakers) prevent the students either to understand the question correctly or to answer properly using the competence bases scheme.

The general problems can only be solved by more practice in reading and listening competence in the subject mother language at a former status. The involved students are aged between 16 – 18 years old; at this age they should be able to get the content of a specific question properly and to answer at a certain intellectual level.

6.5.5 Multimedia and interactive applications

Mayer (2014) researched, that multimedia messages, containing minimum words and pictures intend to foster learning. The experience from the study results in a confirmation of this finding.

This dual-channel addresses more intensively to human learning. It seems that, following this research, videos or multimedia applications are processed more intensive and contribute to the learning success. On the other hand, a certain saturation with multimedia material can be recognized. Videos are part of everyday life and the attraction of videos or multimedia based simulations is very low due to the mass of watched videos or the games played regularly by the students.

Interactive applications support students who are interested in the context of some processes or to play around and gain some new experience as they help them to learn in an easier way. Other students finish the practical work very quickly due to daily stimulus satiation or simple missing motivation.

A very interesting feedback came from a focus round in which the students asked why they should strain themselves to find out something that the teacher is knowing and could tell them in simply words. This statement is completely controversy to the idealistic idea that students want to learn by trying out something on their own.

Obviously the learning economy and the missing endeavour to be actively involved in the learning process is dominating the behaviour of several students. From these findings it is necessary to undertake intensive research how nowadays students like to learn and in which way the use of multimedia, interactive applications or a learner-centered approach really works.

6.5.6 Assessment and grading

The continuous formative assessment was performed stringently and consequently. Measuring the contributions to activities and the involvement of students lead to a sufficient result. Additional assessments focusing on the reflection of complete chapters made it easy to come to grades satisfying both students and the teacher.

The formative assessment can be done easily in smaller groups (this means approximately 20 students). In bigger groups it is not so easy to have the necessary frequency of talking to students and to take the necessary notes about the students' work performed.

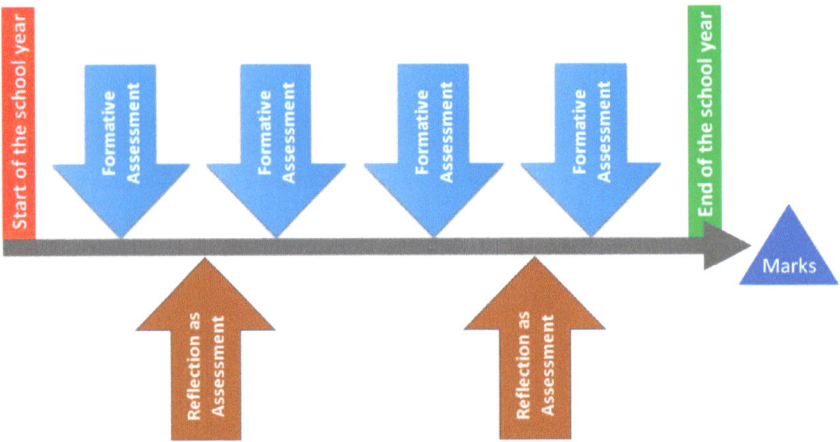

Figure 50: *Continuous assessment as executed during class*

It is absolutely necessary to know each of the students or to identify the involved people (in bigger groups by badges), otherwise it is impossible to perform this continuous formative assessment. In bigger groups, it is difficult to take notes in simply lists. In such a case, other forms of assessment and notes dealing with the assessments must be found. In groups with more than 30 students, formative continuous assessment seems to be impossible and should be replaced by other frequently done assessment methods.

Formative assessment is also time consuming and therefore the time factor also forces to shift to alternative assessment methods.

6.5.7 Evaluation of the teaching

The evaluation of the teaching was done by a survey asking the students and regularly reflection of the teacher. The results of the survey are part of the book.

The reflection focused on several items, like the quality and enhancement of quality of the teaching, the material provided to the students and the used multimedia material during class. During the last year, teaching in three different age groups, important findings appeared and were taken into account for the improvement of the method.

Enhancement of active teaching

One item is the enhancing of active involvement and more intensive use of activities performed in small groups of three. The higher level of active involvement combined with a high performance in presentation of the group work enables interested students to increase their problem solving capacity, the deeper understanding of specific processes and problems as well as a more intensive learning process during class. The observation of less interested students indicates that less motivated students, who do not use the offer of active participation, have disadvantages in the learning and either need additional learning time at home or perform poorly in grading. The students are at an age in which they can decide on their own how intensive they want to participate actively during class and how ambitious they are. The problem of these students is missing "real" motivation, they see learning as a kind of duty to get their annual report and are not interested to do more as necessary to survive class. Solutions must be found for these students to increase the motivation even if it is not clear how it can be done in this context.

More multimedia material and interactive material

Students like to watch short and informative videos and to try out something. To produce short videos a simple video editor is necessary to bring the essentials of videos to a short sequence lasting finally for 2 – 5 minutes. Material is available from many American universities (in English language) and could be used for this purpose. It is the working time and experience of the teacher to care for these videos. Here a bigger group of teachers preparing the material is an advantage. The provision of appropriate material should be the duty of the department (or of the school).

6.6 Problems with the Infrastructure

Two problems in context with the school can be identified in using the teaching method: Missing material for the hands-on experiments and technical problems of the ICT environment.

6.6.1 Missing technical equipment for hands-on experiments

The curriculum defines a strict plan for the learning goals defined as a competence-based framework. This means that the learning goals are used to define the 18 topics, which are relevant for the final exams. Therefore, it is clear which basic and fundamental experiments students should have seen or performed during the three years of attending physics lessons. These experiments should be analysed and the necessary equipment for them should be available in the physics lab. If something is broken the related equipment should be replaced so the teacher can perform the essential experiments without problems.

6.6.2 ICT problems

Problems using ICT are evident and well known. It must be distinguished between problems in context with students' equipment and others in depending on the infrastructure of the school.

Students' problem

Students are responsible for their own devices. The owners must solve upcoming problems with the equipment and generally, the teacher is not in charge to solve these problems. If the problems are in context with the teaching environment it is necessary to solve these problems immediately, otherwise the affected student cannot follow class anymore.
Typical situations are a broken network connection, failure in accessing the learning platform, or failure in printing a document. These situations must be solved as quickly as possible.

Infrastructure problems

The teacher must handle these situations. Often problems emerge in fields in which the teacher has no influence or power to solve them.
Typical situations are broken Internet connection, broken wireless LAN, broken projector or other similar technical obstacles. Teachers are forced to improvise and to make the best out of the situation.

6.7 What Students Need

The reflection of the teaching, the feedback from the students and the discussion with colleagues results in some considerations about missing students' skills, abilities and knowledge. These can be classified in more or less six categories. They cover simple skills to organize their learning as well as complex issues like approach to learning, to define goals, to provide the necessary attitude, or simply to have some motivation to learn.

Figure 51: *Students' Needs*

Many of the mentioned items can be taught in an earlier stage (for example primary high school) and should be part of the general education before the students enter the stage at secondary education.

6.7.1 Time management

For students it is necessary to have an excellent time management to terminate a teaching year successfully. This includes for example scheduling for assessments as well as the sense for prioritizing and properly handling of the collected material. So students have to decide which material is the most important for their learning or reflections for the next assessment and to develop a sense for efficient and time economic learning.

6.7.2 Managing learning resources

Time management stays in context with the management of the resources, both human and physical. Human resources mean to contact the teacher to get answers to open questions as well as to be assisted in finding or downloading needed material. This covers as well the capacity to be able to use the technology as the own capacity and power to process the own learning.

6.7.3 Learning activities

Students must be able to have a clear view to the sense of the learning activities. For the students, it must be obvious that their impact to the various learning activities contribute to their learning success.

From the observation during class it seemed that students prefer to attend class, keep restrained in their activities and to learn only before dedicated assignments.

Due to the continuous formative evaluation, these students finish class with low level of grades and the achievement of their competences in the subject is marginal.

6.7.4 Learning environment

Many students are not familiar enough with the learning environment. It is necessary to bring the students to an acceptable and equal level as quickly as possible after the start of class. In many cases the obstacles can be found in the missing computer literacy. Erstad (2010) mentions that the idea of a digital generation which can perfectly handle media and technical devices is overgeneralizing and gives the impression that all young people today are super-users and highly competent in their use of different media. The same situation is in the field of digital literacy and therefore it is necessary to care for an efficient and sustainable education in using multiple devices and the related software.

6.7.5 Attitude

The fact mentioned at the learning activities has the reason in low motivation. Adult learners attending courses normally have a high level of motivation and they have clear goals. Adolescent students in general education often miss this motivation and therefore they only try to "survive class" reaching the minimum level of competence.

Students involved in the described teaching are in an age in which they need to see some value for them to perform requested tasks (Hudson, 2016). The resulting lack of skills and knowledge leads to deficits which play an important role as a disadvantage for following education. This logical chain was not clear for many of the observed students (and still is not).

Also, the endurance to be involved actively in class, to contribute to discussions or other activities, often lacks and leads to a lower level of learning success. Another typical obstacle to reach a high level of competences is the strategy of minimizing the effort in class, preparation work and continuous learning.

It is a typical result of the teacher's personal observation of students that these people with high level of motivation, long lasting endurance and high level of engagement and effort did best in learning success within the last five years.

The attitude is a key to understand various problems mentioned in 6.5. and must be seen as a means to amend the issues listed there.

6.7.6 Goal setting

Students have to set goals. These aims often are in context with their future plans, for example dealing with their further education. For many students, these aims are missing and they attend and follow class as "their duty", to follow the wish of their parents, or from other motivation.

These goals for the learning, the view to needs in future education and other issues in context of motivation should be available due to the (beginning) maturity of the learners.

Students missing these mentioned items are not so successful in their learning and need support from parents, family (and maybe more mature friends) to set their goals, to prioritize their needs and have a clear view of the importance of successfully learning for their future.

7 Transferability Guide

Generalizability and transferability are two related, but different issues that should be discussed in the frame of a versatile use of results from this study. In this chapter proposals are given for the generalizability of the findings, the focus is laid on the technical point of view, the different subjects and the different fields of education.

The different fields of education compare the findings from School Education with the settings in Higher Education (HE) and Adult Education (AE).

The transferability is discussed as well considering the possible fields of a transfer of the teaching method.

The basic precondition to transfer the described teaching method is the use of a multiple device by all attending students as described before.

7.1 Pedagogical Approach

In chapter 2 a summary of various methods and pedagogical approaches are mentioned as a source of the specific elements selected and used for the presented teaching method. The idea behind was to use the most appropriate pedagogical access picked out of the available theory, in some way "Taking out the best".

To transfer the described method to different teaching fields or environments it is absolute necessary to use a learner-centered approach. Wolf (2012) describes in her manuscript the necessary culture shift in teaching in the United States. She analyses the diversity of the students' population in higher education and recommends learner-centered instructions in a learner-centered environment. This coincides exactly with the experience taken within the last six years.

Each transfer of the method obviously should follow the idea of a learner-centered teaching. This can be realized in all the addressed fields of learning, school education as well as higher education or adult education. Respecting the necessary learning economy (especially in time related issues) it is also possible to practice a learner-centered approach in vocational education and training.

7.2 Versatile use in Different Fields of Education

School Education differs partly from Higher Education and completely from Adult Education. The core difference makes the age of the learners, and the maturity (connected in most cases with the age). Another aspect is the life experience of elder people and the advantage of pre-knowledge and the routine of learning.

7.2.1 Higher Education

The situation in Higher Education is similar to School Education. The learners are older, but have a similar background, similar experience and also more or less the same pre-knowledge. Basically all traditional students (studying to continue their education after having passed the Secondary Education) are digital natives and should be familiar with the use of the computer, the related programs and the creating of notes for their learning process. Most students own their own multiple device and can use it in the lectures or other teaching events.

From this point of view, the teaching model can be transferred 1:1 to higher education.

Another aspect is the necessary impact from the university (or teaching organisation).

- **Technical issues**
  The teaching institution has to care for the access to a network, for the necessary eLearning platform and the technical preconditions in the lecture hall (like electric power supply and WiFi access points in the necessary number).
- **Organisational issues**
  Students must be instructed how to use the method, where to find the basic material and how the distance learning repository can be used for learning at the begin of their studies.

An important item is note-taking. Many students never learned an efficient way to take their notes and therefore often do not know what is important for their learning.

Universities normally do not provide user drives at their network for all students. Therefore, the access to material must be foreseen by a learning platform or something similar. This platform must be a central access point for the students to find all the necessary material or links to further resources. Tzimopoulos et alt. (2015) mention in their study that it is crucial for learners to have one well defined access to a virtual learning system and the material should not be split into packages provided at different web-based resources.

The described teaching method offers a way to leave simple lecturer-driven lessons and to switch to more student activity including a well-proven system to take notes. The method can be transferred easily for lectures with a huge number of students. The bigger the number of students the more difficult seems the active involvement.

7.2.2 Adult education

Adult education can be seen completely different compared with school education. The differences start with the teaching or training conditions. Most courses in Adult Education are short courses fixed on a specific topic or competence. The living situation is also differently than the one of students. Most adults are employed and attend the training or the teaching event parallel to their work, often in evening hours or blocked at the weekend. For many of them learning economy is crucial, the time factor is of high relevance and a massive focus on efficient reaching of the learning goals is visible. Knowles (2005) assumes that adult learners are more internally motivated and problem-oriented as well as they are more self-directed than students in School Education or Higher Education (Straka, 2000).

Possible problems may arise from the use of multiple devices. Giannoukos et alt. (2015) found out in their case study for a small typical Greek town that for adults the use of computers is natural in their daily life and that the questioned sample is quite well educated in computer literacy. "Concerning the determination of the familiarity of adults with a series of simple computing applications, the findings are ambiguous. In some applications …" can be found in their conclusion. That means that a trainer may expect some computer literacy in the group of adult learners. Nevertheless, the trainer needs to check the availability of the requested skills and it is necessary to instruct the learners (if necessary). These basic instructions must be taken into account if planning a course using the described method of technology enhanced Training.

Another issue is the provision of the necessary infrastructure which must be available. This covers a WLAN network with Internet access and the facilities to distribute the content.

Gorges (2012) found similarities between adult learners and students in higher education. Both demand self-directed learning and therefore should be open to an efficient learner-centered teaching.

7.2.3 Vocational education and training

A transfer to vocational education is basically possible, especially in a training situation similar to school education. This means longer lasting courses in a well-equipped environment as described before.

A special challenge is the (continuous or further) vocational training. Most people in professional life do not have so much time or do not want to spend much time for their vocational training. They require effectiveness of the training, they are interested to gain the necessary competences as quickly and efficiently as possible.

For this group of learners, the presented training method is a practicable way of effective training. People in professional life are accustomed to computers as daily tools in their work. The necessary computer literacy can be assumed as well as the necessary routine to use the required computer software. If the fitting learning environment, like WLAN and the process of delivering the basic content, is given the presented training method can be seen as a promising way for further or continuous education.

7.3 Subject Related Issues

From the basic structure, the teaching method is independent from the taught subject. Nevertheless, it was developed with a special focus on teaching science, namely physics. To transfer the method and to adapt it individually specific issues must be taken into account.

The most differences arise in language teaching. The various techniques of teaching, the approach to speak and practice the language, the many options of active teaching using an intensive student-centered approach make the use of multiple devices appear in a different sight and from a different perspective.

In the following discussions several typical subjects are presented and a description of possible changes or obstacles is done.

7.3.1 Mathematics

Teaching mathematics is in close context of calculation and practical hands-on activities mixed with explanation of mathematical theory. The approach to teach mathematics using multiple devices offers a broader scope of active learning by more team work, individual example solving or other typical learner-centered activities.

Calculating by using handwriting is an appropriate way in learning mathematics but messes the note-taking by mixing electronical notes with handwritten documents. To use multiple devices consequently in mathematics special programs are needed. These tools must be used to do the calculation and to create the necessary documentation as well. Such a tool is, for example, MathCad[22], a commercial solution, or Maple and several other tools.

Another option is to use tools like GeoGebra[23] parallel to a text document, to copy the relevant parts (as graphics) into the text document and to save

---

[22] MathCad was developed by Mathsoft and sold 2004 to Parametric Technology. It offers the combination of calculation inside a document which covers also the text notes taken by the students. More information is available at the webpage http://www.ptc.com/engineering-math-software/mathcad

[23] Geogebra was developed by Markus Hohenwarter as a student's project at the University of Salzburg and is an open-source project coordinated by the University of

the calculation work in a GeoGebra file. This assumes a high level of knowledge and discipline from the students. The missing possibility to leave comments in the GeoGebra documents is a big disadvantage. Therefore, this combination is far from the best practice but an acceptable compromise. In any case, it forces a high level of ICT knowledge and handling of the programs of the students and a much higher level of experience from the teachers.

Finally, Maxima should be mentioned as a sophisticated tool with a huge scope of functionality. An obstacle is the complicated input method and the high level of learning to use the program properly. As described above the tool can be used parallel to the note-taking by inserting calculations and results into the document.

Summarizing it seems that no satisfying acceptable and affordable solution exist for taking notes in mathematics by a simple combination of programs. Beneath the mentioned products there exist other tools, like Maple[24] (promoted as "The Essential Tool for Mathematics"), or Scientific WorkPlace[25], which is available in several versions for taking notes including a calculation program.

7.3.2 Chemistry

Teaching chemistry shows similarities to teaching physics. A problem occurs in taking notes. Chemical formulas cannot be handled as easy as mathematical formulas which are relevant in physics. There is no affordable system available (2016) which can be used easily by the students. The typical word processing programs do not supply chemical formulas and the available add-ons are unsatisfying. To provide formulas as graphics is necessary for the advantage of personally taken notes for the students.

On the other hand, several online platforms providing content and multimedia material exist and supply the teacher in performing a learner-centered teaching with special students' activities.

Linz (Austria). The program can be downloaded from the webpage http://www.geogebra.org/

[24] http://www.maplesoft.com/products/Maple/

[25] http://www.mackichan.com/

Hands-on experiments in the lab are also an appropriate way to involve students actively.

7.3.3 Biology

The described system was developed for science teaching and therefore can be transferred easily to teach biology. The distribution of material works the same and other issues like multimedia material and simulations can be used in an equitable way.

An obstacle could be the problem of chemical formulas – as this is often an issue in biological content.

7.3.4 Geography

Teaching geography can be counted to scientific subjects also. Differences occur in specific activities as mentioned by Morgan (2012) like case studies or processing statistics. For these activities, the use of multiple devices is an advantage and findings or activity results can be inserted easily into the taken notes.

7.3.5 Languages

Language teaching differs from teaching science. Taking notes to specific matters will work the same way as in science teaching. The multimedia support for watching videos or other related multimedia-based content is similar to teaching physics.

Other issues, like vocabulary or grammar, will need additional tools or software. Language teaching does not use so strict patterns as the teaching of a fixed curriculum as in science teaching. Therefore, additional strategies for teaching must be developed. Group discussions can be recorded easily with a multiple device.

Practical use of language by speaking is a crucial issue in language learning. In these situations, the multiple device does not play an important role; students have to concentrate on their speaking and listening.

For assignments or assessments, technical devices can be used as useful tools (for example in cloze test to evaluate the understanding of oral texts).

Language teaching needs other concepts as mentioned and presented before for technology enhanced teaching.

7.3.6 History, philosophy, psychology, ethics

All these subjects can use the presented method more or less without bigger changes.

The well-developed system to take notes including the material, which should be used by the students, ensures a high quality of personal notes. The multimedia features of multiple devices supply the lessons in an efficient way.

7.4 Related Software

The described teaching method used a special office software (Microsoft Office), which is available for the students as a general licence of the Austrian Ministry of Education. This software is always necessary to be able to work on a computer, but often the software is not available or too expansive. Here is a list of the used software and optional software as freeware or under a GNU licence. A list of the software sources is provided in the appendix to the book.

Type of software	Used software	Alternative software (examples)
Word processor	Microsoft Word®	Libre Writer26
		Open Office Writer27
Image Processing	Paint.NET	GIMP
Video Viewer	Windows Media Player	VLC Media Player
	VLC Media Player28	
PDF viewer	Acrobat Reader DC	

Table 21: Overview of the used software

---

[26] Also available for Apple Operating Systems and Linux
[27] Also available for Apple Operating Systems and Linux
[28] This is an option for students using Windows 10®.

It is clear that each fitting software which is fulfilling the requirements can be used.

The features of the software and the requirements of the subject to the software are a sophisticated issue. Due to a list of concrete requirements the decision about the used software must be done.

7.5 eLearning Platform

The eLearning platform is foreseen as a means for distribution of the basic texts for class as well as for competence tests. The minimum requirement of the platform is the functionality of a repository. This includes the following features:

- Password protected access to the platform
- Easy system to retrieve the texts (good structure of the repository)

The used eLearning platform was a Moodle 3.X server and can be replaced by a good cloud-based repository to provide the used files in an appropriate structure.

Competence checks can be done electronically by using interactive PDF documents. They can be provided in the repository, downloaded by the students, compiled, renamed, and finally uploaded as individual files in the repository. From here the teacher or trainer may download the documents and assess them.

The use of an eLearning platform like Moodle requires a high level of competence of the teacher or trainer. This covers the knowledge about the creation of a well-structured course, the implementation of the competence checks based on closed and open questions and the evaluation of the competence checks. In cases of a not in the institutions own intranet integrated Moodle server the necessary web space, the maintenance of the server and related activities including the competences are all necessary to be handled.

7.6 Assessment

Assessment gives the teacher or trainer information about the students' knowledge and learning. Besides this, assessment is necessary to fulfil the criteria to grade the students or learners in the frame of their educational field. Grades for students at high school level are replaced in Higher education by credits (in Europe for example by ETCS) or ECVET in Vocational education and training.

7.6.1 Formative assessment

The standard in education is a formative education which results either in grades (in School education) or otherwise in the mentioned ETCS or ECVET. The expected results must be defined fitting to the current definitions of ETCS or ECVET. Positive evaluation automatically ends in the foreseen credits. For adult education assessments are also necessary, but in this field of education the mentioned credits may not exist and can be replaced by certificates.

7.6.2 Individual solutions

In adult education, other assessment methods can be considered due to the course topic and course implementation. The method must be planned and structured in any case during the development of the course structure and must be published to the course participants in time (best at the beginning of the course).
It is clear that a certain type of recognition of the training must be foreseen and integrated in the course for adult education.

7.7 Blended Learning

The presented method is suitable to be used in Blended Learning. Blended Learning mixes onsite teaching with distance learning. Distance learning is always technology based. In the onsite teaching parts of Blended Learning as the described method and framework can easily be implemented using a 1:1 transfer.

8 References

Ackerman, Elise (2013): The bring-your-own-device dilemma. In *IEEE Spectrum* 50 (8).

Altherr, Stefan; Wagner, Bodo Eckert; Jodl, Hans J ̈org (2003): Multimedia material for teaching physics (search, evaluation and examples). In *European Journal of Physics* 25 (1), pp. 7–14. Available online at http://iopscience.iop.org/article/10.1088/0143-0807/25/1/002, checked on 7/20/2016.

Ayres, Paaul; Sweller, John (2005): The Split-Attention Principle in Multimedia Learning. In Richard E. Mayer (Ed.): THE CAMBRIDGE HANDBOOK OF MULTIMEDIA LEARNING. New York: Cambridge University Press, pp. 135–146.

Barer-Stein, Thelma; Draper, James A. (1993): The Craft of teaching adults. Enl. ed. Toronto: Culture Concepts.

Bates, Tony; Poole, Gary (2003): Effective teaching with technology in higher education. Foundations for success. 1st ed. San Francisco, CA: Jossey-Bass (The Jossey-Bass higher and adult education series).

Ben-Jacob, Marion G.; Ben-Jacob, Tyler E. (2013): Perspectives on Online and On-Site Pedagogy: The Impact of Technology Now and in the Future. In *Art and Design Review* 1 (1), pp. 1–5, checked on 1/12/2016.

Biggs, John; Tang, Catherine (2007): Teaching for Quality Learning at University. What the Student Does. 978 0 335 22126 4: Open University Press/McGraw-Hill Education, checked on 2/3/2016.

Bloom, Benjamin S.; Füner, Eugen (1976): Taxonomie von Lernzielen im kognitiven Bereich. 5. Aufl. Weinheim u.a.: Beltz (Beltz-Studienbuch, 35).

Boch, Françoise; Piolat, Annie (2005): Note Taking and Learning: A Summary of Research. In *The WAC Journal*, pp. 101–113, checked on 4/24/2016.

Brame, Cynthia J. (2015): Effective educational videos. Vanderbilt University. Available online at https://cft.vanderbilt.edu/guides-sub-pages/effective-educational-videos/.

Branch, Robert Maribe (2008): Instructional design. The ADDIE approach. New York, London: Springer.

Cardellini, Liberato (2002): AN INTERVIEW WITH RICHARD M. FELDER. In *Journal of Science Education* 3 (2), pp. 62–65, checked on 1/25/2016.

Carlson, Maura O'Brien; Humphrey, Gregg E.; Reinhardt, Karen (2003): Weaving science inquiry and continuous assessment. Using formative assessment to improve learning. Thousand Oaks, Calif.: Corwin Press.

Carlson, Maura O'Brien; Humphrey, Gregg E.; Reinhardt, Karen (2003): Weaving science inquiry and continuous assessment. Using formative assessment to improve learning. Thousand Oaks, Calif.: Corwin Press.

Chuang, Yea-Ru (1999): Teaching in a Multimedia Computer Environment: A Study of the Effects of Learning Style, Gender, and Math Achievement. In *Interactive Multimedia Electronic: Electronic Journal of Computer Enhanced Learning* 1 (1). Available online at http://www.imej.wfu.edu/articles/1999/1/10/index.asp, checked on 1/24/2016.

Clark, Ruth Colvin; Lyons, Chopeta C. (2011): Graphics for learning. Proven guidelines for planning, designing, and evaluating visuals in training materials. 2nd ed. San Francisco: Pfeiffer (Pfeiffer essential resources for training and HR professionals).

Dick, Walter; Carey, Lou.; Carey, James O. (2015): The systematic design of instruction. Eighth edition. Boston: Pearson.

Erstad, Ola (2010): Educating the Digital Generation. Exploring Media Literacy for the 21st Century. In *Nordic Journal of Digital Literacy* 5 (01), pp. 56–71. Available online at https://www.idunn.no/dk/2010/01/art05, checked on 6/9/2016.

European Commission (2007): Key Competences for Lifelong Learning. European Reference Framework. Directorate-General for Education and Culture. Bruxelles. Available online at https://www.erasmusplus.org.uk/file/272/download, checked on 2/2/2016.

Gagné, Robert M. (2004): Principles of instructional design. With assistance of Walter W. Wager, Katharine Golas, John M. Keller. Princeton, N.J.: Cengage Learning, Inc.

Giannoukos, Georgios; Besas, Georgios; Hioctour, Vasilios; Georgas, Thomas (2016): A study on the role of computers in adult education. In *Educ. Res. Rev.* 11 (9), pp. 907–923. DOI: 10.5897/ERR2016.2688.

Gordon, Neil (2014): Flexible Pedagogies: technology-enhanced learning. Flexible Pedagogies: preparing for the future. In *The Higher Education Academy*. Available online at https://www.heacademy.ac.uk/system/files/resources/tel_report_0.pdf, checked on 10/1/2016.

Gorges, Julia; Kandler, Christian (2012): Adults' learning motivation. Expectancy of success, value, and the role of affective memories. In *Learning and Individual Differences* 22 (5), pp. 610–617. DOI: 10.1016/j.lindif.2011.09.016.

Gross, Gail (2014): How Boys and Girls Learn Differently. HuffPost, checked on 5/4/2016.

Guo, Philip (Published on: 2013): Optimal Video Length for Student Engagement. In *eDx*, Published on: 11/13/2013. Available online at http://blog.edx.org/optimal-video-length-student-engagement.

Guri-Rosenblit, Sarah; Gros, Begoña (2011): E-Learning: Confusing Terminology, Research Gaps and Inherent Challenges. In *International Journal of E-Learning & Distance Education* 25 (1), checked on 7/20/2016.

Hasan, Aalia (2014): Using Technology in the Classroom (EdTechReview). Available online at http://edtechreview.in/trends-insights/insights/1460-how-technology-can-enhance-classroom-teaching.

Hawkins, Mike (2010): Help Them Retain What You Train. In *training*. Available online at http://www.cedma-europe.org/newsletter articles/Training Magazine/Help Them Retain What You Train Oct 2010 29.pdf, checked on 4/25/2016.

Hofmann, Peter (2008): LEARNING TO LEARN: A KEY-COMPETENCE FOR ALL ADULTS?! In *Convergence* 41 (2), pp. 173–181. Available online at http://search.proquest.com/openview/231b05a99a9db2ec7f8311751e1fbc25/1.pdf?pq-origsite=gscholar.

Hoskins, Bryony; Fredriksson, Ulf (2008): Learning to Learn: What is it and can it be measured? Ispra (VA), Italy. Available online at http://www.jrc.ec.europa.eu/, checked on 7/15/2016.

Howe, Michael J. A. (2006): The Utility of Taking Notes as an Aid to Learning. In *Educational Research* 16 (3), pp. 222–227.

Hudson, Chris (2016): The 7 Secrets of Motivating Teenagers • Understanding Teenagers Blog. Edited by Chris Hudson. Available online at http://understandingteenagers.com.au/blog/the-7-secrets-of-motivating-teenagers/, checked on 6/10/2016.

Jabbarifar, Taghi (2009): The importance of classroom assessment and evaluation in educational system. In: 4th International Conference on Teaching and Learning. International Conference of Teaching and Learning. Malaysia, 16.11. Malaysia. Available online at https://my.laureate.net/Faculty/docs/Faculty Documents/INTI Conferences/Parallel Sessions 4/4C/4C-03-P142 Iran .pdf.

Khan, Mohid (2010): Richard M. Felder - an autor, an educator … a legend. In *Chemical Engeneering & Science Magazine* 01 (01), pp. 40–48. Available online at http://www4.ncsu.edu/unity/lockers/users/f/felder/public/Papers/RMF_interview(BUET).pdf, checked on 9/24/2016.

Kirkpatrick, James D. (2016): Kirkpatricks four levels of training evaluation: ATD Press.

Knowles, Malcolm S. (1989): The making of an adult educator. An autobiographical journey. 1st ed. San Francisco, Calif.: Jossey-Bass (A Joint publication in the Jossey-Bass higher education series and the Jossey-Bass management series).

Krathwohl, David R. (2002): A Revision of Bloom's Taxonomy: An Overview. In *Theory into Practice* 41 (4), pp. 212–225, checked on 1/25/2016.

Laughlin, Patrick R.; Hatch, Erin C.; Silver, Jonathan S.; Boh, Lee (2006): Groups perform better than the best individuals on letters-to-numbers problems: effects of group size. In *Journal of personality and social psychology* 90 (4), pp. 644–651. DOI: 10.1037/0022-3514.90.4.644.

Ledesma, Patrick (2011): The Ideal Technology Device for Students and Teachers - Leading from the Classroom - Education Week Teacher, checked on 4/23/2016.

Mayer, Richard E. (2014): Cognitive Theory of Multimedia Learning. In Richard E. Mayer (Ed.): The Cambridge Handbook of Multimedia, pp. 31–48.

Mayer, Richard E. (Ed.) (2014): The Cambridge Handbook of Multimedia. Cambridge University Press.

Mazohl, Peter (2015): Quality in Blended Learning. Concepts for a quality framework in blended learning. Wiener Neustadt: P. Mazohl (Eigenverl.).

Mazohl, Peter (2016): Technology Enhanced Teaching. With assistance of Harald Makl. In: 9th Annual International Conference of Education, Research and Innovation. Seville, November, 14 - 16. International Academy of Technology, Education and Development. Seville: IATED.

Mazohl, Peter (2016): Students' feedback to technology enhanced teaching. Wiener Neustadt. Document.

Mazohl, Peter; Makl, Harald (Eds.) (2015): Blended Learning Quality – Concepts Optimized for Adult Education. BladEdu Consortium. Wiener Neustadt: Mag. Peter Mazohl, checked on 4/25/2016.

Meyer, Hilbert (2014): The German Tradition of Didactics and Recent Research Findings about Teaching and Learning. Shanghai International Curriculum Forum. Shanghai, 11.2014. Available online at http://www.schulpaedagogik-heute.de/conimg/Archiv/SH_11/06_02.pdf, checked on 1/25/2016.

Mills, John; Glover, Chris (2006): Who Provides the Feedback - Self and Peer Assessment? Formative Assessment in Science Teaching (FAST) project. In *Formative Assessment in Science Teaching*. Available online at
https://www.open.ac.uk/fast/pdfs/Mills and Glover.pdf, checked on 1/22/2016.

MIT Teaching and Learning Laboratory (2015): Assessment and Evaluation. Available online at http://tll.mit.edu/assessment/assessment-and-evaluation, checked on 9/24/2016.

Moore, Cathy (2013): Action mapping: A visual approach to training design. Let's save the world from boring training. Available online at http://blog.cathy-moore.com/action-mapping-a-visual-approach-to-training-design/, updated on 1/18/2016, checked on 1/18/2016.

Morgan, John (2012): Teaching secondary geography as if the planet matters. Abingdon, Oxon, New York: Routledge (Teaching school subjects as if the planet matters).

Morrison, Gary R.; Ross, Steven M.; Kemp, Jerrold E. (2004): Designing effective instruction. 4th ed. Hoboken, NJ: J. Wiley & Sons (Wiley/Jossey-Bass education).

Naidu, Som (2003): Learning & teaching with technology. Principles and practices. London, Sterling, VA: Kogan Page (Open & flexible learning series).

Petersen, Pia Melchior; Tønnesen, Lone Guldbrandt (2005): TEACHING: DIDACTIC ISSUES IN ODL. In Koen DePryck, Jens Vermeersch, Rachel Savage (Eds.): Getting started in ODL. Antwerpen, Apeldoorn: Garant.

Prensky, Marc (2001): Digital Natives, Digital Immigrants. In *On the Horizon (MCB University Press* 9 (5)), checked on 4/22/2016.

Romando, Richard (2007): Motivation Theory. ezinearticles. Available online at http://ezinearticles.com/?Motivation-Theory&id=410700, checked on 4/17/2016.

Rožman, Laura; Koren, Andrej (2013): Learning to Learn as a Key Competence and Setting Learning Goals. In Valerij Dermol, Nada Trunk Širca, Goran Đaković (Eds.): Active citizenship by knowledge management & innovation. Proceedings of the Management, Knowledge and Learning International Conference 2013, 19-21 June 2013, Zadar, Croatia. Bangkok, Celje, Lublin: ToKnowPress (MakeLearn), pp. 1211–1218. Available online at http://www.toknowpress.net/ISBN/978-961-6914-02-4/papers/ML13-388.pdf.

Schunk, Dale H.; Pintrich, Paul R.; Meece, Judith L. (2008): Motivation in education. Theory, research, and applications. 3rd ed. Upper Saddle River, N.J.: Pearson/Merrill Prentice Hall.

Smirnova, Ludmila (2008): Technology Enhanced Teaching and Learning for Student (and Teacher) Success. In *Faculty Resource Network New York University,* checked on 4/22/2016.

Steinberg, Brian (2012.): Study: Young Consumers Switch Media 27 Times An Hour, 4/9/2012. Available online at http://adage.com/article/news/study-young-consumers-switch-media-27-times-hour/234008/.

Stöger, Heidrun (2012): Mädchen und Frauen in MINT. Bedingungen von Geschlechtsunterschieden und Interventionsmöglichkeiten. 1. Aufl. Münster: LIT (Lehr-Lern-Forschung, 1).

Straka, Gerald A. (2000): Conceptions of self-directed learning. Theoretical and conceptional considerations. Münster, New York: Waxmann.

Tzimopoulos, Nikolaos; Filioglou, Michail (2015): The course itself. Blended learning courses and tutorial support. In Peter Mazohl, Harald Makl (Eds.): Blended learning Quality – Concepts Optimized for Adult Education. Wiener Neustadt: Mag. Peter Mazohl, pp. 56–93. Available online at http://www.blendedlearning-quality.net/typo3/fileadmin/user_upload/project_results/pdf/99%20BladEdu%20documentation%20EN%20Ver%2005.pdf.

Walvoord, Barbara E. Fassler (2010): Assessment clear and simple. A practical guide for institutions, departments, and general education. Second edition. San Francisco, CA: Jossey-Bass (Jossey-Bass higher education series).

Weatherhead, Rob (2014): Say it quick, say it well – the attention span of a modern internet consumer, 2/28/2014. Available online at https://www.theguardian.com/media-network/media-network-blog/2012/mar/19/attention-span-internet-consumer.

Weimer, Maryellen (2013): Learner-centered teaching. Five key changes to practice. Second edition. San Francisco, CA: Jossey-Bass, A Wiley Imprint.

Wilson, Leslie Owen (2013): Anderson and Krathwohl - Bloom's Taxonomy Revised - The Second Principle. Anderson and Krathwohl – Understanding the New Version of Bloom's Taxonomy. Available online at http://thesecondprinciple.com/teaching-essentials/beyond-bloom-cognitive-taxonomy-revised/, checked on 1/25/2016.

Wolf, Mary Ann: Culture Shift: Teaching in a Learner-Centered Environment Powered by Digital Learning. Available online at
http://all4ed.org/wp-content/uploads/2013/10/CultureShift.pdf.

Other Publications from the Author

Quality in Blended Learning
Peter **Mazohl**

Blending Learning is a teaching reality in the education landscape. There exist several books dealing with the implementation of Blended learning courses. What is missing is a well-defined quality assurance system based on an appropriate quality framework.

This book defines a quality framework for Blended Learning, based on the existing ISO/IEC standard, by enhancing this standard with a special focus on the learner's needs. The book gives an overview, how this quality framework looks like, describes the context to Blended Learning and includes practical advices about the implementation.

ISBN: 978-3-901679-19-3

Blended Learning Quality – Concepts Optimized for Adult Education
Edited and published by Peter **Mazohl**

Blended Learning is a relatively new teaching method, which emerged in the last 8 years. Developed as a combination of classroom teaching and distance learning, this method takes up an important role in the educational system. Big companies were the first to use this teaching and training concept because they expected cost reductions. Nowadays the first research work about the efficiency and the necessary environment of Blended Learning are published. One of the issues mentioned is a missing quality concept for Blended Learning. This documentation gives an overview of the project's results.

You may order the book here: Peter Mazohl, H.O. Staglgasse 13, A-2700 Wiener Neustadt, Austria, or at www.amazon.uk (in English language)

www.ingramcontent.com/pod-product-compliance
Lightning Source LLC
Chambersburg PA
CBHW041541220426
43664CB00002B/19